9/66

POOR LANDS,
RICH LANDS

The Widening Gap

STUDIES IN
ECONOMICS

Consulting Editor:
WILLIAM LETWIN
Massachusetts Institute
of Technology

POOR LANDS,
RICH LANDS

The Widening Gap

L. J. ZIMMERMAN

Institute of Social Studies, The Hague

RANDOM HOUSE/NEW YORK

FIRST PRINTING

© *Copyright, 1965, by Random House, Inc.*

PREFACE

This book is based on a series of lectures I have given during the last few years at the Institute of Social Studies in The Hague. They are illustrated and refined with the help of examples from the studies of several of the course participants. The synthesis of these many experiences, my own and others, form the content of this book.

I want to thank Mr. A. K. Atallah (Lebanon), Mr. F. M. O'Carrol (Ireland), Miss S. Clemhout (Belgium), Miss V. Escala (Panama), Mr. Z. Y. Hershlag (Israel), Mr. Z. Joueijati (Syria), Mr. M. H. Kahn (Pakistan), Mr. E. F. Lari (Italy), Miss L. M. Mantey (Mexico), Mr. H. Onoe (Japan), and Mr. W. L. Posthumus (Canada) for the use I have made of their research during their stay at the Institute. I am also very grateful for the excellent editorial help I received from Mrs. M. Z. Klipper of Random House.

L. J. Zimmerman
Institute of Social Studies
The Hague
The Netherlands

September 1964

CONTENTS

POOR LANDS,
RICH LANDS

The Widening Gap

Chapter 1

INTRODUCTION

The term *economically underdeveloped* area probably made its first public appearance at United Nations gatherings in 1944 and 1945. Before this date, the fraternity of experts used to talk about *colonial areas* or *backward areas,* and the classical political economist would speak of the "progress of society" as a universal concept in the form of a linear time scale on which any economic system may be located.

Although the new term may be expedient in politics, it would be a mistake to suppose that it is a useful tool in economic analysis. One agrees with Arthur Hazlewood [1] when he states that neither the term *underdeveloped areas* nor its connotation commands universal agreement, but not when he adds that its denotation, however, is tolerably clear—and that no generally accepted alternative term seems to be available. On the contrary, the term is rather confusing.

Underdevelopment has been explained in terms of too small a supply of social overhead capital, that is, roads, ports, power plants, etc. (Rosenstein-Rodan); in terms of a disproportion of productive factors—i.e., of labor, land, capital, mining resources, etc. (Papi); and, more generally, in terms of the disequalizing factors caused by the maldistribution of economic activities (Myint). Perhaps somewhat more to the point, however, is the definition in terms of a relatively low ratio of capital and entrepreneurship to other factors of production, but with reasonably good prospects that additional capital can be profitably invested (McLeod).

But the words "somewhat more to the point" require elucidation. S. H. Frankel is right in saying that it will depend on the specific criteria of development applied by the observer, and on the position adopted by him, whether a society is regarded as economically developed or underdeveloped. In other words, it is very important to remember that statistical compilations used to compare developed and underdeveloped areas may well reflect the value scales of the already developed areas.[2]

When all this is taken into consideration, it appears that H. W. Singer was the nearest to the truth in saying that an underdeveloped country is like a giraffe: it is difficult to describe, but you always know it when you see one. But since it is somewhat difficult to give our giraffe a decent place in our economic toolbox, the best thing we might do in economic theory is to drop the concept of underdevelopment completely and reserve it for politicians, who really know how to handle it. Consider, for example, President Truman's Point Four definition saying that underdeveloped areas are those areas where more than half the people of the world are living in conditions approaching misery, where food is inadequate, disease rampant, where economic life is primitive and stagnant, and where poverty is a lasting and dangerous handicap.

As far as economic analysis is concerned, we are on much safer ground when we speak of countries with a relatively low or a relatively high per capita income. Firstly, this has the advantage that we are dealing from the very beginning with a measurable concept; secondly, it becomes immediately clear that no sharp borderline can be drawn between rich countries on the one hand (say the United States) and very poor (say India) on the other, but that we will find all kinds of gradations in between. In the third place, our definition seems to have the advantage of attracting attention to the differences in per capita income—that is, the characteristics of low-per-capita-income countries appear not as a prologue but as an epilogue of our analysis.

Although we will thus focus our attention on differences in per capita income from area to area, it is still more important to explain the differentials in the increment of per capita income from country to country. The interest shown in this particular subject will be clear after reading Chapter 2, in which it is demonstrated that the discrepancy between the rich and the poor countries has become much greater during the past century. One does not need much political imagination to understand that this is one of the greatest political problems our generation will have to solve.

It is the purpose of this book therefore to *analyze the factors affecting the increase in per capita income* on the one hand and, on the other, to *find an explanation for the huge differences in these increments from area to area and from period to period.*

CHANGING APPROACHES TO ECONOMIC PROGRESS

After lying almost dormant for about a century, interest in the conditions of economic progress[3] revived after World War II. To understand this, one first has to realize that in science those things that are presumably self-evident are normally of no interest to scientists. On the contrary, scholars are interested in precisely those phenomena that are supposed to be inexplicable.

In the history of economic thought, we may, roughly speaking, distinguish three epochs in which the economist's approach to economic progress differs fundamentally. Although the selection of dates is somewhat arbitrary, we suggest 1830 and 1930 as milestones in this development. In the period preceding 1830—i.e., during the classical epoch—economists wrote nothing but Inquiries into the Nature and Causes of the Misery of Nations.[4] During the century between 1830 and 1930, the belief in economic progress was so great that it was postulated instead of analyzed in economic theory. The third period, World War I, and especially the World Crisis of the 1930s, meant the end of the belief in an unbridled economic progress. After World War II economists as well as politicians began to realize that practi-

cally everything that had been said in the past about
economic progress referred to Western countries alone.
As soon as they had realized this, they understood also
that they were confronted with a problem that had
much more in common with the truculent *political economy* of Smith, Ricardo, and Marx than with the har-
monic *economics* of Marshall. After a careful study,
H. W. Singer even came to the conclusion that Marxian
analysis, in which rising standards of living for given
groups and sections are somehow held to be compatible
with general deterioration and impoverishment, is much
more true for the international scene than it is for the
domestic one.[5] In Chapter 2 we will see to what extent
this statement is correct, but let us first give a brief
sketch of the three periods mentioned above.

In the first epoch—i.e., the period prior to 1830—the
fundamental problem puzzling the classical economists
was how the increasing population of Western Europe
could be fed. According to Adam Smith, countries are
populous not in proportion to the number of people
whom their produce can clothe and lodge, but in proportion to the number they can feed. When food is provided, it is easy to find the necessary clothing and lodg-
ing. But though the latter are at hand, it may often be
difficult to find food.[6]

For the first time in the history of mankind, classical
economists were confronted with a sharp increase in
population. Although demographic data earlier than
1800 are very inaccurate indeed, we may assume that
in the first century A. D. world population was about 250
million. It took about 1500 years for the world population to double. In the seventeenth century an accelera-
tion in the increase in population set in, and we may
assume that the population increase observed by classical economists was at least twice that of the population
increment known to have occurred in the past. Gregory
King, an excellent demographer in his day, estimated
the population of Great Britain in 1696 at 5.5 million,
and he thought that it would take about 600 years to

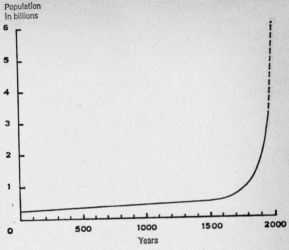

FIG. I.I   World Population

double it. Fifty years later Süssmilch already estimated that it would take only about 100 years to double the European population.

The great question for all classical economists then was: How can we, with a given acreage of fertile land, feed this increase of population? With the increase of population there were two alternatives: agricultural workers (representing about 80 per cent of the population of Western Europe) would individually receive a smaller acreage of fertile land, or soils of an inferior quality would have to be brought under the plow.

ANNUAL INCREASE IN POPULATION IN PER CENT IN EUROPE, AMERICA, OCEANIA, AND THE ASIATIC PART OF THE U.S.S.R.[7]

1650-1750	0.3
1750-1800	0.7
1800-1850	0.9
1850-1900	1.1
1900-1950	1.0

Without going into the details of the law of diminishing returns—one of the cornerstones of the classical theory—it will be clear that under the conditions described above, assuming that we do not introduce the concept of technological progress, sooner or later the addition of a new unit of food will require a greater amount of labor. Thus, according to the then current labor theory of value, food, measured in units of labor, would become more and more expensive. Ricardo demonstrated, therefore, that the rent of land would increase, and because he supposed as all other classical economists did that real wages would equal the subsistence level, he came to the following general prognostication of the distribution of national income: constant wages, increasing rent, and falling profits. But as the funds destined for the payment of wages—the so-called wage fund—had to be financed out of these profits, in the long run no more capital would be available to finance the employment of additional labor. Thus the increase of population would have to come to a standstill and stagnation would set in.[8]

According to some authors of this period, diminishing returns in agriculture could be balanced or perhaps even be surpassed by increasing returns, through the use of machinery in industry. But as the raw materials employed in industry all were produced under the law of diminishing returns (technological progress once again being left out of consideration), the maximum one might hope to reach was to keep per capita income constant with a long-term increase in population.[9]

One might remark that Ricardo was aware of the fact that the natural tendency of profits to fall is happily checked at repeated intervals by improvements in machinery,[10] but this is the exact opposite of the approach we find in the following epoch—i.e., the conviction that there will always be profits because there will always be innovations. On the other hand, Ricardo feared that the improvements in technology might turn out to be too laborsaving, thus causing unemployment.[11]

Therefore, we may say with Schumpeter that, at the end of the eighteenth and the beginning of the nineteenth century, economists and humanitarians were pessimistic and doubtful about what sort of future capitalistic production would provide for humanity at large.[12]

To understand this attitude one has to realize first of all that the philosophers in Western Europe had thought for centuries that the culture and wealth of ancient Rome might perhaps one day be reached, but would never be surpassed. Before discarding such an idea as old-fashioned, we should remind all Western-centered economists that M. I. Rostovtzeff (1870-1952), one of the greatest students of the ancient world, has stated that the wealth of ancient Rome was surpassed only by Western Europe and the United States in the nineteenth and twentieth centuries (but not with reference to the beauty of the towns).[13]

Although quite a number of authors from as early as the end of the seventeenth century, might be quoted who thought that the human mind had made essential progress in the past (e.g., Fontenelle and Swift),[14] it was not before the end of the eighteenth century that men like Condorcet and Godwin bluntly stated that in the future not only might mankind increase, but per capita income might increase as well. It was especially against these optimists that Malthus launched his attack, and it was Malthusian thoughts, not Godwinian, that characterized classical economic thinking. Although Malthus was utterly mistaken so far as Western Europe and the United States are concerned, he was without doubt much nearer to the truth in terms of the world as a whole than were his optimistic opponents.

Singer says: "In terms of world income, the situation has probably deteriorated during the last three generations in respect to all three of Pigou's criteria: average size, equality of distribution, and stability over time. If we define the 'average' world income as that of the median world citizen, the spectacular improvement which has occurred at one extreme and which has fascinated economists and other observers becomes irrelevant." [15] (Compare however, Chapter 2.)

In the second place, one has to realize that up to 1800 the average European was a peasant and, generally speaking, his techniques of production had not changed for centuries.[16] From the time of ancient Rome to the nineteenth century, most scholars believed that all countries were predestined to pass from (1) primitive life supported by free gifts of nature, through (2) pastoral life, to (3) agriculture. This concept may be traced back to Varro, a Roman scholar of the first century B.C. For Varro, the agricultural economy was the highest conceivable form of economic civilization, and urban crafts appeared as superstructures of agriculture. Not until the end of the eighteenth century did urban crafts and trade reach such an importance that, so far as the Western countries were concerned, it became necessary to extend Varro's classification by adding industry and trade as an economic stage succeeding agriculture (as did Friedrich List.)[17] At the same time the introduction of turnip husbandry caused an agrarian revolution in Great Britain because it tended to displace the three-field system and obviated the necessity of fallowing every third year, thus increasing available arable land by, roughly speaking, 50 per cent.

John Stuart Mill, the last of the great classical economists,[18] knew all this, but being brought up entirely in the classical tradition and influenced by the writings of the French socialists he could not but interpret these facts as events that held in check, even during long periods, the law of diminishing returns. However, if we know that during the first half of the nineteenth century, with all the tremendous changes brought about, the mass of the English people barely succeeded in maintaining real per capita income constant,[19] we may understand Mill's pessimistic view that "it is questionable if all the mechanical inventions yet made have lightened the day's toil of any human being. They have enabled a greater population to live the same life of drudgery and imprisonment, and an increased number of manufacturers and others to make fortunes. They have increased the comforts of the middle class. But they have not yet begun to effect those great changes in human destiny, which it is in their nature and in their futurity to accomplish." But while Mill was writing, the general trend in economic thought was already changing; and it was the belief in technological progress, not in diminishing returns, that called the tune during the next generation.

So far as the second, the optimistic, period is concerned, we are not far from the truth when we locate its beginning around the year 1830. Of course, not everyone was pessimistic until this year and optimistic afterwards, but the year more or less indicates a turning point in the general trend.

1830 was chosen in the first place because it was the year in which Thomas Babington Macaulay published a most interesting article in the January issue of the *Edinburgh Review*. In this article we find opinions completely opposed to those of the classical economists, who thought that although technological progress might temporarily check the law of diminishing returns, in the long run the situation for the world would become more and more difficult. Against such opinions Macaulay wrote: "We cannot absolutely prove that those are in error who tell us that society has reached a turning-point, that we have seen our best days. *But so said all who came before us* [italics added], and with just as much apparent reason. . . . On what principle is it that, when we see nothing but improvement behind us, we are expected to see nothing but deterioration before us? . . . If we were to prophesy that in the year 1930 a population of fifty million, better fed, clad and lodged than the English of our time, will cover these islands . . . that machinery constructed on principles yet undiscovered will be in every house, that there will be no highways but railroads, no travelling but by steam, that our debt, vast as it seems to us, will appear to our grandchildren a trifling encumbrance, which might easily be paid off in a year or two, many people would think us insane. . . ."

But the year 1830 was chosen in the second place because it was the year in which Auguste Comte published the first part of his *Cours de philosophie positive*.* The cornerstone of Comte's positive philosophy is his law of human progress, which states that each of our leading conceptions—each branch of our knowledge—passes successively through three different theoretical conditions: the Theological, or fictitious; the Metaphysical, or abstract; and the Scientific, or positive. Through Comte the idea of progress became familiar in the social sciences, but Comte had borrowed it from his friend Saint-Simon, and it was the latter who had already written at the beginning of the nineteenth century that the law of progress was for the social sciences what the law of gravitation was for the natural sciences. In opposition to those who thought that technological progress might from time to time check the tendency of profits to fall, Saint-Simon stated that entrepreneurs (*les industriels*) regulate progress.[20]

By and by people started to see the fundamental difference between the feudal system, which was static by nature, and capitalism, which lives by the grace of continuous change—not only so far as economic life is concerned, but for social life as a whole. The change from liberal to social democracy is as essential to capitalism as the change from the steam engine to the electric motor. It is for this reason that the capitalisms of, say, 1850, 1900, and 1960 have only their dynamics in common, not their external appearances. It is one of the ironies of history that none other than Karl Marx stated

---

* It might also be mentioned that in 1830 Charles Lyell published the first volume of his *Principles of Geology*, in which he developed the thesis that changes in the earth's crust as the geologist observes them in the middle of layers of earth are not the results of sudden calamities, but have to be understood *as an evolutionary process of progress*, which began a long time ago and is still going on.

in the Preface of the first volume of his *Das Kapital:* "The present Society is no solid crystal, but an organism capable of change, and it is constantly changing."

Sociologists and economists like Werner Sombart, Max Weber, and Joseph Schumpeter[21] have drawn attention to the fact that capitalism has, as a condition of life, a continual flow of technological and social changes, and can live only in a cultural climate that accepts and assimilates those changes relatively easily. Perhaps the most amazing feature of capitalism in the past hundred years has been that its social organization has generally succeeded in overcoming those tensions that were felt at every moment between the existing social desiderata and the technological and political possibilities within the same generation. It is for this reason that communism, despite Marx's economic prognosis, failed to obtain a foothold in highly developed capitalist countries but on the contrary scored its successes in those countries that did not develop the capitalistic dynamics.

As far as economic theory is concerned, once the faith and confidence in continual change became part and parcel of the Western pattern of culture, the economists took economic change and economic progress for granted. For the first time in history, historical data were so much in harmony with this conviction (as long as we confine our attention to the Western world) that economists simply postulated economic progress. The big problem remained to explain why progress did not increase at a constant rate but in a sequence of periods of prosperity and depression.[22] Thus the problem of the business cycle made its appearance on the stage and with it the problems of partial and general equilibrium —because business-cycle theory explains the deviations from an equilibrium situation. When classical economists discussed the stationary state, they discussed a real situation—a situation they expected would materialize, in which profits would have disappeared, population would be constant, and the level of living would be at a minimum. For the economists of the last part of the nineteenth and the beginning of the twentieth century, however, the stationary state was nothing but a tool of analysis, a cerebral experiment. It was not a prognostication of a future state of affairs, but a point of departure to explain deviations from the equilibrium— i.e., business cycles. The more these topics became the fundamental problem of economics, the more the upward moving trend in all kinds of macroeconomic time series was taken for granted; thus no one complained when, for example, in all econometric models not the time series themselves but the percentage deviations from their trends were introduced. During this period economsits analyzed the accelerations and the retardations of the upward-moving trend, but not the trend movement itself.

Even Schumpeter's famous theory of economic development is, after all, not a theory of development because the innovations, the prime movers in his theoretical model, are treated as an exogeneous factor.[23]

We cannot terminate this brief survey of the optimistic epoch without saying a few words about Karl Marx, one of the most fascinating scholars in the field of social change. As far as the future of capitalism is concerned, Marx shared the views of the classical economists, especially Ricardo. He was convinced of the tendency of profits to fall, and believed furthermore that once a very high degree of development had been attained, capitalism would break down. Marx did not consider the possibility of technological progress as a means of holding diminishing returns in check; to him it was a treadmill for capitalists—they must run even faster just to stand still, for technological progress must always keep one step ahead of the rate of capital accumulation.[24]

In the Marxian system, technological progress is considered inseparable from processes by which it is accompanied and which it sets in motion—processes that Marx expected to lead to a downward trend in profit rates as well as to very unfavorable wage trends.[25] We do not need to go into the details of Marx's laws of accumulation, concentration, and impoverishment here: Marx supposes that capitalism will "wither away."

But it is not a pessimistic conclusion that Marx draws from this analysis. On the contrary, he believes that by historical necessity capitalism is doomed, and that the same held true for all earlier social organizations. But because the idea of progress is written into the very constitution of the (materialistic) dialectics and because Marx used this method for his interpretation of history, he introduced, without any special emphasis on his part, the unexpressed but essential implication that the revolutionary development of society is always a lawlike movement toward better things.[26]

In the middle of the nineteenth century Marx did not and perhaps could not see that the propensity to accept social and technological change in capitalism is much greater than it had been in all earlier societies. In the Preface of the first edition of *Das Kapital* Marx draws attention to the fact that the high officials in the United Kingdom as well as in the United States at that time were already aware that the prevailing relationship between labor and capital could not continue in the long run, and that radical changes were badly needed. This, Marx saw correctly, did not mean that miracles could be expected in the short run, but it demonstrated that the ruling class of those days—and this too Marx correctly observed—understood that capitalism was an organism capable of change, and was constantly changing. Marx did not fail so far as his demonstration of the untenable nature of the existing order of the society was concerned, but he completely underestimated the capacity of adaptation of that same society to the social needs that arose. He did not foresee what E. H. Carr calls the "permanent social revolution." According to Carr, this social revolution became a worldwide phenomenon in the twentieth century; the Russian revolution was a symptom and a part of it.[27]

Today practically all economists agree that the impoverishment observed by Marx is not a logical consequence of capitalism itself, but was caused by rapid economic development—a development that had to be financed at heavy cost, and was largely paid for by the laborers.[28]

Although the choice of the year 1830 as turning point from pessimism to optimism may be open to controversy, many will agree that about 1930 a new pessimistic trend in Western thought set in. The breakdown of the League of Nations, together with the economic world crisis, made faith in world peace and eternal prosperity disappear like snow before the sun. It was (and may still be) a period of general cultural pessimism.[29] Thus we should not be astonished when we find after 1930 a revival of the classical theory of declining profits. We find the idea developed, for example, in Keynes's *General Theory of Employment, Interest and Money*. According to Keynes,[30] during the nineteenth century the growth of population and of invention, the opening up of new lands, the state of confidence, and the frequency of war over the average decade seem to have been sufficient (taken in conjunction with the propensity to consume) to establish a schedule of the marginal efficiency of capital which allowed a reasonably satisfactory average level of employment to be compatible with the rate of interest—high enough to be psychologically acceptable to the rich. The modest rates of interest over a period of almost 150 years encouraged a rate of investment consistent with an average of employment which was not intolerably low. Keynes supposes, however, that this has changed fundamentally in modern times (i.e., after 1930); so far as one can guess at the schedules of the marginal efficiency of capital corresponding to increasing amounts of capital, the rate of interest is likely to fall steadily.[31]

Thus far, therefore, Keynes is in agreement with Ricardo and with Marx, but from this point onwards Keynes does not take a pessimistic attitude. He thought that the fall of the rate of interest might be the most sensible way of *gradually** getting rid of many of the objectionable features of capitalism: a man would still be free to accumulate his earned income with a view to spending it at a later date, but his accumulation would not grow.[32] This stagnation thesis was based on the assumption that the scarcity in the factors of production which cooperate with capital has become too great to be offset by technological and organizational improvements.[33]

Today we are rather far away from Keynes's Utopia, where the marginal efficiency of capital as a result of the steady accumulation of capital and the lack in innovations will be equal to zero. For the time being, the highly developed capitalistic countries all struggle with inflationary, not deflationary pressures, and in many of them the percentage increase in national income is greater than it has ever been before. Without doubt Keynes was correct in stating that the typically long-run rate of interest is rather low in the leading financial centers, and has been so for at least the past century,[34] but he forgot that this holds true only for the Western world. However, in at least one half of the world the marginal efficiency of capital is higher than in the developed countries. But institutional factors militate against a flow of capital to such areas, because private loans always are given for specific projects, and those projects are usually profitable only when considerable additional infrastructural investments are made. Private lenders are not willing to invest their money in the latter projects. Only after international organizations—like the International Bank for Development and Reconstruction—have financed those infrastructural investments will the rich countries become the source of free capital flows and thus have the power to "even up" returns throughout the world, provided political stability prevails in the underdeveloped countries.

The fundamental political problem we thus have to

* Italics added to indicate fundamental difference with Marx.

solve is how to channel these savings to the areas where
they are really needed most. As soon as we realize a
sound international political integration, the objective
preconditions for the optimal allocation of the available
savings throughout the world would be fulfilled,* with
the result that the long-term bogey of economic maturity would disappear completely.

Although Keynes's thoughts did not go in this direction, one has to see in the General Theory one of the
fountainheads of modern economic thought so far as the
problems of economic progress of the low-per-capita-
income countries are concerned.[35] His influence in this
respect has been much greater than this last paragraph
suggests. I have already indicated that scholars are interested only in phenomena that are not self-evident.
As for the business cycle, everyone agrees today that its
cause is the discrepancy between total supply and effective demand; as long as we are speaking about pure
theory we all know the instruments with which an inflationary—or a deflationary—gap might be overcome. Today the main problem is no longer what kind
of instrument should be chosen, but how it is possible in
an actual situation to realize such an economic policy.
Yet after all this is not a problem of economic theory;
it belongs to the domain of the political scientist and the
public administrator. As far as the economist *pur sang*
is concerned, he might consider the problem solved—
for the time being at least.

I suppose that this is one of the deeper causes why
so many economists in the postwar period try to
sharpen their wits on so-called development problems
—i.e., on the dynamics of supply and not (in the first
place) on effective demand. At the same time this may
explain why economists are less eager than they have

---

* On purpose we wrote the "objective preconditions," because the examples of the South in the United States and the
Southern part of Italy demonstrate that political unity alone
is not a sufficient condition to develop retarded areas: the economic *climate* in such areas has to be created deliberately.

been in the past to eliminate trends, but on the contrary are interested precisely in the problem of how those trends might be explained.

Finally, it seems of importance to indicate that it was Keynes who drew the economists' attention to the importance of the concept of national income as a tool of economic analysis. To a certain extent it was his influence that made the United Nations sponsor so many inquiries into the national and the per capita incomes of many countries all over the world.

We shall return to these inquiries in the next chapter. For the moment, we may say that it has been demonstrated that the inequalities in the distribution of "world income" are much greater than the inequalities found so far within any national economy.

A DEFINITION OF TERMS

We have stated earlier that our purpose in this book is to analyze the factors affecting the increase in per capita income, and to find an explanation for the huge differences in those increments from area to area and from period to period. Let us finish the present chapter with three definitions that will give, at the same time, an indication of the design of this study.

We shall speak of *economic growth* as taking place when the long-term percentage increase in total output (in national income) is equal to the long-term percentage increase in population. Economic growth thus indicates a constant real per capita income with a growing population—i.e., the Malthusian case (Chapter 4).

We shall speak of *economic progress*[36] as occurring when the trend of the percentage increase in total output is greater than the trend of the percentage increase in population. Thus economic progress indicates a long-term increase in real per capita income—i.e., the Western case in the past 150 years (Chapter 6).

We may take for granted that in each country where we observe economic progress today there has previ-

ously existed a situation of economic growth. Therefore there must have been a time of transition in the
past, a period of perhaps a few decades in which
fundamental changes in the entire social life must
have occurred. We shall speak of *economic development* where we are concerned with this relatively short
period of transition from economic growth to economic
progress—i.e., the contemporary case of many of the
poorer countries (Chapter 5). Thus we have defined
economic growth, development, and progress in an un-
ambiguous way.[37] In Chapter 2 we shall demonstrate
that our definitions, so far as the growth situation and
the progress situation are concerned, enable us to divide
the world in two parts according to our criteria. However, during the rest of our analysis the reader will
see that we did not make our definitions merely for the
sake of classifications, but on methodological grounds
as well. It is not difficult to explain the growth situation
with the aid of a simple Harrod-Domar model (Chapter
4), and the progress situation also lends itself to a purely
economic analysis (Chapter 6). Economic development
however, confronts us with a different kind of problem:
it is a situation in which the constants and the parameter
of our growth model change rather suddenly. We may
describe such shifts (Chapter 5), but the economist will
soon find that many noneconomic factors—e.g., political, sociological and sociopsychological—have caused
those shifts. There our explanation of the development
situation will be less analytical and more descriptive
than our explanation of the processes of economic
growth and economic progress. Because thus far we
have seen that national and per capita income play a
role of paramount importance in our analysis, let us
first examine how they have changed in the past hundred years in various parts of the world.

NOTES

1. A. Hazelwood, *The Economics of Underdeveloped Areas* (1954), p. ix.

2. S. H. Frankel, *The Economic Impact on Underdeveloped Societies* (1953), Chaps. 3 and 4.

3. This phrase was used as the title of Colin Clark's classic in this field, published originally in 1941 (2d ed. 1951, 3d ed. 1957).

4. Compare J. Bonar, *Philosophy and Political Economy* (1922), p. 211.

5. H. W. Singer, "Economic Progress in Underdeveloped Countries," *Social Research*, March 1949, p. 2.

6. Adam Smith, *Wealth of Nations* (1776), Chap. XI, p. 2.

7. *The Determinants and Consequences of Population Trends*, United Nations (1953), p. 12.

8. Compare especially D. Ricardo, *Principles of Political Economy and Taxation* (1817), Chap. VI.

9. John Stuart Mill, *Principles of Political Economy* (editor W. J. Ashley), Book I, Chaps. 10-13.

10. Ricardo, *op. cit.*, Chap. VI.

11. *Principles,* Chap. XXXI (added in the third edition).

12. J. Schumpeter, *History of Economic Analysis* (1954), p. 461.

13. M. I. Rostovtzeff, *A History of the Ancient World* (1926), Vol. II, Chap. XX.

14. Compare R. V. Sampson, *Progress in the Age of Reason* (1956).

15. H. W. Singer, *op. cit.*, p. 2.

16. Compare W. Sombart, *Der moderne Kapitalismus* (1902), Vol. II, 2, p. 650. "In 1800 people in the country-side in Europe lived in about the same conditions as in 800, or if we take into consideration the increase in the exchange relations, as in 1300."

17. Compare W. S. Woytinsky and E. S. Woytinsky, *World Population and Production* (1953), p. 413. It is important to indicate in this context that when Smith speaks occasionally about the "application of machinery" he mentions the plough, the ship of a sailor, the mill of a fuller and the loom of a weaver, none of them much more recent in-

ventions than the plough. (Compare W. Stark, *The History of Economics* (1944), p. 31.)

18. Or rather the economist who showed within his writings all the conflict of mid-nineteenth century opinion; compare John Stuart Mill, *Principles of Political Economy* (ed. Ashley), Book I, Chap. XII, p. 3.

19. *Theories of Economic Growth,* edited by B. F. Hoselitz (1960), p. 126.

20. Compare Henri de Saint-Simon, *Lettres d'un Habitant de Genève à ses Contemporains* (1803).

21. Werner Sombart, *Der moderne Kapitalismus* (1902); Max Weber, *Gesammelte Aufsätze zur Sozial und Wirtschaftsgeschichte* (1924); Joseph Schumpeter, *Theorie der wirtschaftliche Entwicklung* (1912).

22. Compare A. Javary, *De l'Idée de Progres* (1851), p. 74: "From the beginning of this century the idea of progress has in effect established itself in such a way that in principle it is no longer contested by anyone, and the only question that remains to be pursued is that concerning the conditions in which it is realized."

23. Compare J. Steindl, *Maturity and Stagnation in American Capitalism* (1952), p. 132.

24. B. Higgins, *Economic Development, Problems, Principles and Policies* (1959), p. 116.

25. W. Fellner, "Marxian Hypotheses and Observable Trends under Capitalism: A 'Modernized' Interpretation," *Economic Journal,* March 1957, p. 16.

26. Compare Henry D. Aiken, *The Age of Ideology* (1956), p. 190. In spite of this we do not find in the writings of Marx specific thought on the problems of economic and technological progress in those countries which are referred to today as "underdeveloped." He assumes that not all nations have the same ability for capitalist production. Some primeval peoples (we find in his *Theorien über den Mehrwert,* 1921, Vol. III, p. 519) like the Turks have neither the temperament nor the disposition for it. But these are exceptions. (Quoted from A. Bonne, *Studies in Economic Development,* 1957, p. 245.)

27. E. H. Carr, *The New Society* (1957), p. 87.

28. Compare Chapter 5.

29. Compare K. K. Kurihara, *The Keynesian Theory of Economic Development* (1959), p. 47: "The World Population Conference [of 1954] was reportedly divided into the

diametrically opposed 'pessimistic' and 'optimistic' schools of thought." One even has the impression that in contemporary philosophy it is sometimes difficult to distinguish between optimistic and pessimistic ideas. It is, for instance, difficult to make out if Sartre's statement that "man is condemned to be free" (because his fate is not predetermined), is optimistic—as Sartre assumes himself—or full of pessimism.

30. J. M. Keynes, *General Theory of Employment, Interest and Money* (1936), p. 307.

31. J. M. Keynes, *op. cit.*, p. 375.

32. *Ibid.*, p. 221.

33. *Ibid.*, p. 308.

34. W. Fellner, *Trends and Cycles in Economic Activity* (1956), p. 387.

35. Compare J. P. Henderson, "Contemporary Growth Economics," *Science and Society*, Spring, 1957, p. 136: "Professional economists began to seriously consider the repercussions of the investment process itself a process that required active monetary and fiscal policies not only to ensure that underutilized plant capacity would not develop, but more important, to ensure that growth of the national product would be continuous. With this post-Keynesian shift in emphasis, occurring at the end of World War II, economists stressed the fact that investment was needed not only for its short-run advantages (investment to generate income through the multiplier process) but for the decidedly long-run advantages that accrue—namely the added productive capacity of the economy."

36. It is appropriate to quote here E. H. Carr's definition of progress: "Progress is just what it says, a moving on, a conscious moving on towards purposes which are felt to be worthy of human faith and human endeavor." E. H. Carr, *The New Society* (1957), p. 117.

37. Compare A. J. Youngson, *Possibilities of Economic Progress* (1959), Chap. I.

Chapter 2

THE DISTRIBUTION OF
WORLD INCOME,
1860-1960

Until the Keynesian revolution, most economists were in agreement with Ricardo that "political economy should rather be called an inquiry into the laws which determine the division of the produce of industry among the classes which concur in its formation, than [as Malthus thought] an inquiry into the nature and causes of wealth." [1] Keynes, however, drew the economists' attention to the importance of the concept of national income, and of its formation, as tools of economic analysis. From the middle of the 1930s statistical inquiries into the size of national income have increased vastly and, as previously mentioned, it was Keynes's influence that made the United Nations sponsor so many studies of the national and per capita incomes in industrialized as well as largely agrarian countries all over the world. This is understandable because national income is nothing but a summary of the total flow of goods and services annually available in a country.

PER CAPITA INCOME

Whether we define national income as the total of the economic goods produced by the people comprising a nation, or as the sum total received by these individuals as a remuneration for their contribution in the production of those commodities, or as the sum total of their expenditures (in the widest sense of the word) out of those receipts, in any one of these modes national income is the end product of a country's economic activity.[2]

Dividing national income by the population gives us the per capita contribution in the economic activity. As long as this per capita contribution remains constant over time with an increase in population, we speak of *economic growth;* when we find a positive trend in the per capita contribution we speak of *economic progress.* We have deliberately left welfare criteria out of these definitions; for our purpose concepts like the equality of income or the stability of income over time are of secondary importance; we first must have the cake before we can discuss how to divide it.[3]

If we were to live in a world where the differentials in per capita income and their increments were but small from country to country, it would not be unlikely that income distribution and stability over time would be of paramount importance for a definition of economic progress. But so long as we live in a world where these differentials are enormous, we think that the increase in per capita income as such might be considered as a relatively comprehensive indicator for the increase in the level of living in a country. Thus by trying to find the causes of the differentials in per-capita-income increments, we want to find the causes affecting the differences in the increase in the levels of living, indicating in one way or another the actual living conditions of a people.[4] It was those actual living conditions that John Stuart Mill had in mind when he wrote, in *On Liberty,* that "among the works of man, which human life is rightly employed in perfecting and beautifying, the first in importance surely is man himself."

And because we too are interested in *life as an end product,*[5] we focus on the per capita income, as the totality of resources annually available in a country (divided by the number of people), which gives us a first approximate answer to the question in how far life as an end product surpasses the bare minimum of existence. Thus we can use per capita income on the one

hand as a comprehensive indicator of the ways in which
the available resources of an economy are used, and on
the other hand as an indicator of the level of living.

Although it is rather difficult to estimate national income, it is nevertheless a much easier task than trying to
construct some sort of a comprehensive indicator of the
level of living.

So far as the latter is concerned, the experts mentioned above stopped after having compiled a list of the
most important indicators:

1. Life expectation at birth
2. Infant mortality rate
3. National average food supplies in terms of calories at the retail level compared with estimated
   caloric requirements
4. Proportion of children 5-14 years of age enrolled
   in schools
5. Percentage of population literate, above same appropriate age, total and by sex
6. Proportion of economically active population unemployed
7. Percentage distribution of economically active
   population by principal industrial and occupa-
   tional categories
8. Personal consumption as a proportion of national income

A perusal of this list shows us that (1), (2), and up to
a certain extent (4) and (5) fall under the heading
"life as an end product," or one might call them the
"outputs of the sociocultural process" whereas the others
are the "inputs" in such a process.[6]

Unfortunately, we cannot for the time being measure
these inputs and outputs by the same unit (as is the case
in an input-output matrix of national production), and
therefore it has no operational significance to assume
that in the sociocultural process input equals output.

The only thing one is allowed to say is that total production—and thus per capita income—depends on the inputs in the sociocultural process, and that on the other hand the output of this process depends on total production as well.

Although these sociocultural inputs and outputs thus turn out to be unmanageable concepts, one marginal note in this connection has to be made. The outputs mentioned above are not the results of the inputs in a certain year under consideration, but they are rather the result of previous inputs—i.e., of the integral of inputs. The outputs depend on income (or production), because income is one of the most important factors determining the development of the educational system and of the sociomedical organizations, consisting of hospitals, nurseries, medical care in general, and consultation bureaus.

It is quite possible, therefore, that a country in which national income increases rapidly (because new resources are found) will continue for a rather long period to show relatively low sociocultural outputs, whereas after a war the per capita income can be rather low while sociocultural outputs may be relatively high (because the educational and social services in those countries were organized in a previous and richer period). Table 2.1 illustrates this.

Table 2.1

SOME INDICATORS OF THE LEVEL OF LIVING (1953)

Country	Per Capita Income	Infant Mortality Rate	Life Expectancy at Birth
Sweden	$940	18.7	70.31
Venezuela	500	67.9	—
Netherlands	490	22.1	71.75
Japan	180	48.9	61.27

Although we thus need a great deal of historical data and other information in order to understand the relationship between the per capita income of a specific country and its sociocultural outputs, we found that

those relationships became more regular as we computed the figures for larger economic-geographical
areas. We constructed twelve of these aggregates: (1)
North America, (2) Oceania, (3) Northwest Europe,
(4) Soviet Union, (5) Southeast Europe, (6) Latin
America, (7) Japan, (8) Near East, (9) Far East,
(10) Central Africa, (11) Southeast Asia, and (12)
China.

We know that working with such aggregates is open to
criticism, but one must not forget that everyone accepts
the national and the per capita income of, say, the
United States and India as a statistical notion, although
the per capita income in states like California, Illinois,
and Connecticut is at the moment about twice as high
as that of states like South Carolina, Mississippi, and
North Carolina. Apart from a few great exceptions
(such as Venezuela in Latin America) such differentials
do not exist between the countries aggregated in the
economic-geographical areas mentioned above.

A great advantage of the aggregation, moreover, is
that the areas have populations which usually lend
themselves to more fruitful comparison than the populations of the seventy or eighty countries for which
figures are available. Furthermore, it is not unlikely
that as a result of the aggregation a few of the most
striking idiosyncrasies of individual countries are somewhat cancelled out* and, because we are interested in
long term changes, this is an advantage as well.

Table 2.2 demonstrates this, but it indicates as well
the undeniable interrelationship between per capita income and a few indicators which are most important for
the level of living.† We have chosen these specific indicators because they satisfy rational criteria of value.[7]
One may discuss whether a high or a low birth rate is desirable,[8] and one may even discuss if it is desirable

* This may be the case with a few of the exchange rates as
well.

† In Chapter 3 we shall see that in a great many cases the
same holds true for individual countries as well.

Table 2.2
SOME INDICATORS OF THE LEVEL OF LIVING (1953)

Area	Per Capita Income	Percentage of Economically Active Population Employed in the Primary Sector	Infant Mortality Rate: Number of Deaths in First Year of Life per 1,000 Live Births	Newspaper Consumption in kg per Capita
North America	$1,810	12.7	28.5	32.7
Northwest Europe	680	17.5	36.6	10.0
Soviet Union	500	43.0	48.0	—
Southeast Europe	290	47.3	70.9	—
Latin America	260	51.3	92.5	2.7
Far East	110	65.4	108.7	0.3
Southeast Asia	64	72.3	116.3	0.2

that people live longer, but once a child has been born a low infant mortality is always (in all the social sciences) to be preferred to a higher one.[9] So far as the economic aspect of the problem is concerned, the economist has to judge the money spent upon the child for food, education, etc., as an investment in labor, and this amount has to be written off during the period later on when the child earns an income. (Or to put it in another way, in later life he must earn at least a sufficient sum to enable him to invest the same amount in a newborn child.) If the child dies before it starts working, the whole sum spent on its education and its food is from an economic point of view a bad investment. The higher the infant mortality rate, the higher those bad investments.[10] In one of the other social sciences an opposite outcome does not seem possible.[11]

As for the consumption of newsprint, we take this indicator as the only objective one for the degree of literacy in a country, because it demonstrates to what extent people practice their knowledge of reading.[12] We shall see in Chapter 3 that per capita income and per capita newsprint consumption are highly correlated and since the degree of literacy, or in more general terms the degree of education, is highly correlated with labor productivity as well (see Chapter 6), we are sure that the other social sciences will also come to the conclusion that a higher rate of literacy is desirable for a country.

These digressions were necessary in order to demonstrate that a few important indicators of the level of living show a close relationship with per capita income.

Hence we are allowed to use per capita income as a comprehensive indicator of the level of living, and we are permitted to state, not only in relation to the economic aspects of social life but for social life as a whole, that a higher per capita income is more desirable than a lower one.

INCOME IN RICH AND POOR COUNTRIES

Let us now focus our attention on the distribution of world income as such. Many economists have speculated about the changes in this distribution over the last generations. Starting from the plausible assumption that the increase in income in rich countries is and has been greater (in the rich countries) than in the poor, the conclusion that the inequality in the distribution has increased over time is obvious. As previously mentioned, according to Dr. Singer the situation has probably deteriorated with respect to all three of Pigou's criteria: average size, equality of distribution, and stability over time. Singer further states that if we define the "average" world income as that of the median world citizen, the spectacular improvement which has occurred at one extreme and which has fascinated economists and other observers becomes irrelevant. Later on we will see that our statistical findings do not support Singer's thesis, but let us focus our attention on the distribution of the world income for the period 1952-54.

Professor Theil was perhaps the first to apply Pareto's formula of the distribution of income on the world as a whole, using the United Nation's figures for the year 1949.[13] For the world as a whole, Theil found for 1949 a Pareto coefficient of 0.66, the most unequal distribution of income observed so far.[14] Theil added in his article that even if the incomes of the poorest countries had been largely underestimated—as indeed was the case for China—the distribution of the world income would nevertheless still be the most unequal income distribution thus far observed.

We computed the coefficient for the twelve economic-geographic areas mentioned previously for 1952-54 and found a coefficient of 0.767. Because no population and income estimates prior to 1945 exist for the countries of Central Africa and the Near East (with Egypt and Turkey as exceptions), we also computed the coefficient for the ten remaining areas only. It turned out that the coefficient for these ten areas was practically the same as for the twelve (0.767). Therefore we thought that it was permissible to compute for earlier years the Pareto coefficient for the remaining ten areas and to speak, nevertheless, of the distribution of the *world* income. We must immediately add that this procedure had a certain influence on our findings, because the deleting of

Table 2.3

"WORLD INCOME" FOR TWELVE AND FOR TEN
ECONOMIC-GEOGRAPHIC AREAS FOR 1952-54

	12 Areas	10 Areas
Population, millions	2,425	2,215
Income, billions of dollars	770	750
Per capita income, dollars	320	340

about 3 per cent of the world population means that the per capita income increases by about 6 per cent (Table 2.3). This implies that our estimates for the average income of the world citizen are somewhat upwardly biased. But this will certainly be less than 6 per cent for the year 1860, because we have to assume that the per capita income in the Near East as well as in

Central Africa increased but little in the past hundred years. If one realizes, however, that according to our estimates the average income of the world population —measured in constant dollars of 1953—increased from $90 in 1860 to $430 in 1960, one must agree that this general trend would not have been different had the other two areas been added.

The data for 1960 could be easily computed with the aid of the index numbers of the real per capita income as published by the United Nations. However, the further we went back in the direction of 1860 the less reliable our data became. Even in those countries where statistical research is highly developed, the nineteenth-century income figures must be considered as rough approximations. We think, nevertheless, that the estimates for North America, Oceania, Northwest Europe, the Soviet Union, Japan, and Southeast Asia are rather reliable. The estimate for Southeast Europe had to be made on data concerning three-fourths of its population, but for Latin America and the Far East the situation was still worse. Here the figures prior to 1900 and 1913 respectively are our own estimates, based mainly on the trends we found in other areas. For China, both income and population prior to 1953 had to be estimated. Here too the trends—as well as the absolute levels of the per capita incomes—in the neighboring areas have been used as a compass.

Because we have been engaged in collecting this material for quite some time and have had a rather extensive correspondence with insiders in various parts of the world, we do not think that it will be possible, for the time being, substantially to improve our basic material. We can imagine, however, that someone will consider our ice too thin to skate on. Every Dutchman knows, however, that such a judgment is rather subjective.*

---

* The method of computation is discussed in: L. J. Zimmerman, "The Distribution of World Income, 1860-1960," in *Essays on Unbalanced Growth*, edited by E. de Vries, 1962, and in L. J. Zimmerman, *Arme en Rijke Landen*, 1964.

The final results of our findings are brought together in Table 2.4.

The first amazing (and completely unexpected) result of these findings is the constant and rather high increase in the average world income. But the table also indicates that only very few areas had a percentage increase *above* these averages, hence a first indication for the constancy of the increase in the inequality in the distribution of the world income.

Further, it is interesting to observe that only in Northwest Europe the percentage increase in per capita income has been practically constant over the entire period. All other areas show rather important differentials between the first and the second period. It is unavoidable, of course, that the choice of period influences the results. Had we selected the period 1929-60, we would have found for the Soviet Union an annual percentage increase in per capita income of 4.1, and for the period 1953-60, 8.6.

It has often been stated that the increased inequality in the distribution of the world income has been caused by the fact that the percentage increase in the past in the per capita income in the rich countries has been much greater than it has been in the poorer ones. Table 2.4 shows us, however, that the increase in the per capita income in some of the low-income countries has been considerable in the past. Hence, several of our ten areas have changed place in the column during the last century, as can be seen in Tables 2.5 through 2.7. Thus if we speak of the richest 25 per cent of the world population in 1860, 1913, and 1960, respectively or of the income earned by the median world citizen, we have to realize that in each year different areas are involved. The median world citizen—that is, the one who would be exactly in the middle, if we were to range the people of the various areas according to the average income in every area—has to be sought, in 1860, between the Far East and Southeast Asia (or between $48 and $50), in 1913 between Japan and

Table 2.4

PER CAPITA INCOMES (IN DOLLARS OF 1952-54) AND THEIR PERCENTAGE CHANGES, 1860-1960

Country	Per Capita Incomes			Annual Percentage Change		
	1860	1913	1960	1860-1913	1913-1960	1860-1960
1.0 North America	$420	$1,000	$1,900	1.65	1.41	1.54
2.0 Oceania	440	580	1,020	0.52	1.25	0.84
3.0 Northwest Europe	230	460	860	1.31	1.34	1.33
4.0 Soviet Union	95	160	890	1.00	3.72	2.26
5.0 Southeast Europe	110	200	420	1.14	1.59	1.35
6.0 Latin America	100	160	330	0.89	1.55	1.20
7.0 Japan	40	90	300	1.54	2.59	2.03
9.0 Far East	50	90	120	1.12	0.63	0.89
11.0 Southeast Asia	48	65	70	0.52	0.16	0.38
12.0 China	44	47	110	0.13	1.83	0.92
Total	90	200	400	1.52	1.52	1.52

Table 2.5

DISTRIBUTION OF WORLD INCOME, 1860

	Country	Population, Millions	Income, Billions	Accumulated Figures Population, Millions	Income, Billions	Percentage Distribution Population	Income
2.0	Oceania	1.2	$0.5	1.2	$0.5	0.1	0.5
1.0	North America	34.6	14.4	35.8	14.9	3.2	15.3
3.0	Northwest Europe	122.1	28.5	157.9	43.4	14.3	44.7
5.0	Southeast Europe	86.9	9.5	244.8	52.9	22.2	54.4
6.0	Latin America	37.2	3.7	282.0	56.6	25.5	58.4
4.0	Soviet Union	74.0	7.0	356.0	63.6	32.3	65.4
9.0	Far East	26.0	1.3	382.0	64.9	34.6	66.8
11.0	Southeast Asia	247.0	11.5	629.6	76.4	56.9	78.6
12.0	China	443.4	19.5	1,072.4	95.6	97.1	98.4
7.0	Japan	32.0	1.3	1,104.4	97.2	100.0	100.0

Table 2.6

DISTRIBUTION OF WORLD INCOME, 1913

Country	Population, Millions	Income, Billions	Accumulated Figures		Percentage Distribution	
			Population, Millions	Income, Billions	Population	Income
1.0 North America	99.8	$100.3	99.8	$100.3	6.3	32.9
2.0 Oceania	7.0	4.1	106.8	104.4	6.7	34.3
3.0 Northwest Europe	183.0	84.0	290.5	188.4	18.2	61.8
5.0 Southeast Europe	130.4	26.0	420.9	214.4	26.4	70.3
4.0 Soviet Union	139.0	22.5	559.9	236.9	35.1	77.7
6.0 Latin America	79.5	12.3	639.4	249.2	40.1	81.8
9.0 Far East	61.1	5.7	700.5	254.9	44.0	83.6
7.0 Japan	51.9	4.6	752.4	259.5	47.2	85.1
11.0 Southeast Asia	323.7	21.0	1,076.1	280.5	67.5	92.0
12.0 China	517.4	24.0	1,593.5	304.8	100.0	100.0

Table 2.7
DISTRIBUTION OF WORLD INCOME, 1960

Country	Population, Millions	Income, Billions	Accumulated Figures Population, Millions	Income, Billions	Percentage Distribution Population	Income
1.0 North America	198.5	$376.5	198.5	$376.5	7.9	37.4
2.0 Oceania	12.7	12.9	211.2	389.4	8.0	37.5
4.0 Soviet Union	214.4	190.0	425.6	579.4	16.6	54.9
3.0 Northwest Europe	216.6	185.9	642.2	765.3	25.2	72.3
5.0 Southeast Europe	202.1	84.4	844.3	849.7	33.2	80.0
6.0 Latin America	206.7	68.4	1,051.0	918.1	41.4	86.3
7.0 Japan	93.2	28.0	1,144.2	946.1	45.1	88.8
9.0 Far East	127.3	14.9	1,271.5	961.0	50.2	90.1
12.0 China	683.3	75.6	1,954.8	1,036.6	77.3	97.4
11.0 Southeast Asia	572.3	41.0	2,527.1	1,077.6	100.0	100.0

Southeast Asia (between $65 and $90), and in 1960 between the Far East and Japan (between $120 and $300).

These figures seem to contradict Singer's statement that the increase in the income of the median world citizen has been irrelevant. But whereas some of the areas with a very low income in 1860 also made considerable progress, it is obvious that the inequality in the distribution of the world income increased considerably during the last century. Table 2.8 gives a clear demonstration of this phenomenon, for this table indicates that the 25 per cent of the world population that lived in the lowest income areas of the world in 1860 earned 12.5 per cent of the world income, against 3.2 per cent in 1960.

Table 2.8

PERCENTAGE DISTRIBUTION OF WORLD INCOME EARNED BY 25, 50, AND 75 PER CENT OF THE WORLD POPULATION

Percentage of World Population	*Accumulated Percentage of World Income Earned*		
	1860	1913	1960
25	57.8	68.9	72.1
50	73.3	86.1	90.0
75	87.5	93.9	96.8

Thus we can certainly state that the past hundred years have shown a *relative* impoverishment of the poorest part of our world. As soon as we look at the real income earned by the median world citizen, however, we find that it increased from $50 in 1860 to $300 in 1960. Because the average world income has increased about four times we thus find for our median world citizen a more than proportional increase.

Although Singer underestimated the increase in the income of the median world citizen, the hard fact that the income distribution between the various areas of the world became more and more unequal remains the same. The simplest way to demonstrate this is by using the so-called Lorenz curves. In Fig. 2.1 the diagonal indicates situations where 10 per cent of the world population would earn 10 per cent of the income, 20 per cent of the population, 20 per cent of the income, etc., hence a complete equality in the income distribution.

It is clear that the more the curve bends to the right the more unequal the income distribution will be. Thus Fig. 2.1 indicates a very important increase in the in-

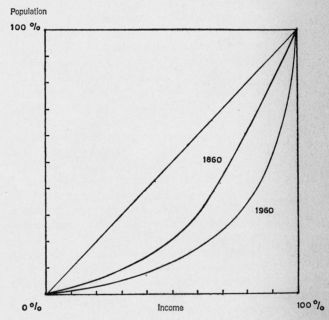

FIG. 2.1   Lorenz curves for world income, 1860 and 1960

equality of distribution of the world income during the past century.

Further, we computed the Pareto coefficient for the period 1860-1960 with the following results:

1860	1.576
1880	1.086
1900	1.006
1913	0.974
1929	0.911
1953	0.766
1960	0.708

Because a lower coefficient indicates a greater inequality in the income distribution, the figures also demonstrate the increase in the inequality. Pareto assumed that a numerical value of 1.5 of the coefficient indicates the "normal" distribution of the national income, and H. T. Davies[15] went so far as to state that a lower numerical value would inaugurate a revolutionary situation (as, according to his opinion, was the case in the years prior to the French revolution of 1789). However this may be, our findings lead to the conclusion that a hundred years ago the distribution of the world income was much more equal than it is today. It goes without saying that today's inequality of income distribution is one of the causes of the huge international tensions of our times.

It is not impossible that, due to the use we have made of the rates of exchange for converting the various national currencies into dollars, certain mistakes have been made so far as the absolute levels of the incomes of the various areas in our base year 1953-54 are concerned. It is even likely that if a better method of conversion had been available for all the countries, the inequality in the income distribution would have been somewhat smaller. (Compare, however, Chapter 3.) But this does not influence our final findings that the income distribution has considerably deteriorated during the last century.

We may now try to draw a few conclusions from our statistical investigations.

First of all, we see that the famous statement of Mandelbaum and of Kuznets—that the rich countries are rich because they were rich to begin with,[16]—holds true so far as North America and Oceania are concerned. Both areas were sparsely populated in 1860 and had an extremely favorable land-man ratio at that time. This lucky event gave these two areas of new settlement an advantage at the start compared with all the other areas. These are also the areas where the increase in population during the last century, respectively 1.76 per cent per annum for North America and 2.49 per cent for Oceania was the greatest in the world.

But Table 2.9 clearly demonstrates that Oceania has now lost the greatest part of its advantage if we compare it with the Soviet Union and with Northwest Europe, whereas the discrepancy between North America and the Soviet Union, impressive as it may still be today, is growing smaller year by year. Also, the gap between Northwest Europe and North America has been declining in the past ten years, due to the high growth rate in Northwest Europe. But it is also interesting to draw attention to the fact that the per capita income of Oceania in 1860 was eleven times as great as that of Japan, against 3.5 times in 1960.

Table 2.9

Country	Per Capita Income, 1860 in dollars	Annual Per Capita Income Increase, 1860-1960 in per cent	Per Capita Income, 1960 in dollars
Soviet Union	95	2.26	$890
Japan	40	2.03	300
North America	420	1.54	1,900
Southeast Europe	110	1.35	420
Northwest Europe	230	1.33	860
Latin America	100	1.20	330
China	44	0.92	110
Far East	50	0.89	120
Oceania	440	0.84	1,020
Southeast Asia	48	0.38	70

This does not mean that the second part of the statement of Mandelbaum—that the poor countries are poor because they were poor to begin with—finds no confirmation in our statistical findings. In Chapter 4 we shall see that this is of paramount importance for our theory of growth.

NOTES

1. D. Ricardo, *Works and Correspondence*, P. Sraffa, ed., Vol. 8, p. 278. Before the publication of his Principles, Ricardo had already written to Malthus that the most important topic in political economy was the progress of a country in wealth and the laws by which the increasing produce is distributed (Vol. 7, p. 24). However, he later on focused his attention to the second part of this statement.

2. Compare S. S. Kuznets, "National Income," in *Readings in the Theory of Income Distribution* (1947), p. 3.

3. However, compare V. Marrama, "The Relationship between the Distribution of Income and Economic Development," *L'Égypte Contemporaine*, July 1955, p. 1.

4. Compare the *Expert Report on International Definition and Measurement of Standards and Levels of Living* (United Nations, 1954), p. 2. The Report further distinguishes between *standards of living*, related to the aspirations of a people—that is, the living conditions which they seek to attain or regain or which they regard as fitting and proper for themselves to enjoy, and the *norm of living*—the desirable conditions of living defined for specific purposes, such as the fixing of minimum wages or working hours as arrived at by national or international agreement. The *standard* and the *norm* which are concerned with what ought to be, serve as a means of evaluating the adequacy of what is—i.e., the *level of living*. Thus the latter, not the former, is of importance for us.

5. Compare N. Buchanan and H. S. Ellis, *Approaches to Economic Development* (1955), p. 7.

6. Because after (3), head (8) has to refer to the capacity to save in the first place, (8) should be headed under the inputs as well.

7. Compare M. Ginsberg, *The Idea of Progress* (1953), p. 43.

8. E.g., economists and military strategists may hold differing opinions.

9. One has to realize that I have here taken the birthrate as a datum. Although I do not deny that under certain conditions a high birthrate may have unfavorable *economic* repercussions, it may also have favorable aspects. An economist can never give the *final* answer.

10. One has to realize that something like 22.5 per cent of the Indian national income is absorbed by the maintenance of children who die before they reach the age of fifteen and thus never get an opportunity of leading a productive life. Compare J. J. Spengler, "The Population Obstacle to Economic Betterment," *American Economic Review*, May 1951, p. 351. We can add here E. Staley's computation (*The Future of Underdeveloped Countries*, 1954, p. 280) according to which the total number of productive years for each 100 live births is approximately 4.750 in the United States and about 1.650 in India. Each birth in the United States thus results in almost three times as many productive adult years as in India.

11. This is of great importance, because, as we indicated already in Note 9, the same cannot be said with relation to a high birth rate as such.

12. This does not need to be the case in the Communist countries, as in those countries advertisements are practically unknown, which partly explains the rather low newsprint consumption in those countries.

13. H. Theil, "Enige kwantitatieve aspecten van het probleem der hulpverlening aan onderontwikkelde landen," *De Economist*, 1953, pp. 721-749. Pareto found his empirical law of income distribution by plotting the logarithms of the number of people N having incomes at or above the level X on the ordinate, and on the abscissa the logarithms of the corresponding incomes. He thus found a series of points $P_1 \ldots P_n$ lying approximately on a straight line. That is, he found that

$$\text{Log } N = \text{Log } A - a \log X$$

or

$$N = \frac{A}{X^a}$$

It will be apparent that the constant A depends on the size of the population and the average level of income. The coefficient α measuring the dispersion of income is independent of the average level of income or the size of population. The α is used as measure of the equality or inequality in income distribution. The numerical gradient of the downward-sloping straight line is equal to the α, and Pareto was convinced that this constant would always, notwithstanding time, place or social structure, be approximately equal to 1.5.

14. Compare Colin Clark, *The Conditions of Economic Progress*, 2 ed. (1957), p. 533, where a great many Pareto coefficients are given, the lowest (1.13) in Clark's table being for the town of Augsburg in 1526.

15. H. T. Davies, *The Analysis of Economic Time Series* (1941).

16. K. Mandelbaum, *The Industrialization of Backward Areas* (1955), p. 4.

Chapter 3

THE ECONOMIC STRUCTURE OF
RICH AND POOR COUNTRIES

In Chapter 2 we have demonstrated that per capita income is a good common denominator of a people's level of living. We may consider income as the sum total of the goods and services produced in an economy (i.e., as the inputs in the economic process), but also as the sum total of the expenditures—consumption and investment (i.e., as the outputs of this process).

Under the first consideration, income is a dependent variable; that is to say, the greater the inputs (labor = L, and capital = K), the greater the national income. We may express this in a simple production function:

$$Y = f(L, K)$$

Under the second consideration income is an independent variable, because, for example, consumption depends on income:

$$C = cY$$

But of course in both cases we are dealing with the same income:

$$\xrightarrow{\quad L \quad} \bigg| \text{National} \bigg| \xrightarrow{\quad C \quad}$$

Inputs   Outputs

$$\xrightarrow{\quad K \quad} \bigg| \text{Income} \bigg| \xrightarrow{\quad I \quad}$$

This simple representation gives the impression that the greater the inputs, the greater the national income and hence the outputs. Without doubt this statement is correct, but we have to add immediately that an increase in output not only depends on the addition of inputs, but on their improvement in quality and change in composition as well. In the present chapter we want to discuss some of these relationships and, because it seems useful, to give a picture of the architecture[1] of economies at different levels of income. Throughout this chapter, let us always take income as the independent variable. We thus pass by in silence the question whether or not a certain structural change is the cause or the effect of a change in income. All we want to show is that in certain cases a very definite interrelationship exists. This seems a legitimate procedure, because it may furnish us with some useful information about what it really means when we say that a country has a per capita income of $200 or $800.

PRIMARY, SECONDARY, AND TERTIARY SECTORS

Let us start this analysis with the shifts in the percentage distribution of employment. We follow here Colin Clark's famous tripartite classification of economic activities in a primary, a secondary, and a tertiary sector. The primary sector comprises agriculture, hunting, and fishing; the secondary, industry, mining, construction, power and the rest, generally the services, are brought together in the tertiary sector.

We have mentioned already that an increase in per capita income goes hand in hand with a decrease of per-

Table 3.1

PERCENTAGE EMPLOYMENT IN THE PRIMARY SECTOR

Country	1830	1870	1910	1960
Great Britain	23	15	8	4
United States	71	51	32	9
Sweden	63	56	48	14
France	63	50	41	25
Japan	—	82	63	33
India	—	—	63	70

centage employment in the primary sector. Table 3.1 clearly demonstrates this general tendency.

An international comparison between per capita income and employment in nonagrarian activities (in order to make the correlation positive) is given in Table 3.2.

Table 3.2

PER CAPITA INCOME AND PERCENTAGE EMPLOYMENT IN THE SECONDARY AND TERTIARY SECTORS

Economic Geographic Area	Year	Per Capita Income, Dollars (1952-54)	Percentage Employment in Secondary and Tertiary Sectors
1. North America	1960	1900	91.0
2. North America	1953	1810	87.3
3. North America	1929	1240	76.6
4. Oceania	1953	960	82.9
5. North America	1913	920	67.3
6. Northwest Europe	1953	680	82.5
7. Oceania	1929	680	75.5
8. Oceania	1913	570	72.8
9. Northwest Europe	1929	530	81.8
10. Northwest Europe	1913	450	76.8
11. Japan	1960	300	67.4
12. Southeast Europe	1953	290	52.7
13. Latin America	1953	260	48.7
14. Far East	1953	110	34.6
15. Southeast Asia	1953	60	27.7

The correlation is rather good and we found the following equation:

$$\log y = 0.0202\,x + 1.3235$$
$$(R = 0.92)$$

where y stands for per capita income and x for the percentage employment in nonagrarian activities.

With the aid of the equation we computed the "theoretical" percentage employment in the secondary and tertiary sectors at a $200 and $800 level, to wit, 48 and 78 per cent.

Kuznets argues that we must be careful as far as causation is concerned: a country is not necessarily poor *because* a great percentage is employed in agriculture. But because the country is poor, capital formation is small and therefore employment opportunities are limited. When income is low, labor has to stay in agriculture with a decline in the land-man ratio and further distress as a result. In India, for example, the land-man ratio declined from 1891 to 1951 from 1.09 to 0.84 acre per man.[3]

But Table 3.1 demonstrates that France and Sweden had in 1830 the same percentage employment in agriculture as India had in 1910, and it was considerably higher in Japan in 1870. In all three countries it diminished considerably, whereas the percentage increased in India. But we can go further and state that at the beginning of the nineteenth century all countries—with only Great Britain as an exception—had about 80 per cent of its population employed in the primary sector. Therefore the thesis that a country is poor because it was poor to begin with is definitely wrong.[4]

But whatever might be the cause, *one* thing is certain: if indeed a decline of percentage employment in agriculture always goes hand in hand with an increase in per capita income, then per capita income in agriculture must be lower than that in the two other sectors.

The figures in Table 3.3 demonstrate this clearly.[5] Due to labor extensive farming, Oceania forms an exception to the golden rule that labor productivity is considerably lower in the primary sector than in the secondary, whereas income in the secondary and tertiary tends to be more or less equal.[6]

Table 3.4, in which Oceania is left out, proves this tendency perhaps more clearly. It has often been assumed that because industrialization tends to diminish disguised unemployment in agriculture, average labor productivity in agriculture will increase faster than in industry. Therefore the tendency for the difference to become smaller should be a characteristic of economic

Table 3.3

PRODUCTION PER LABORER IN THE PRIMARY,
SECONDARY, AND TERTIARY SECTORS (ABOUT 1953)

Economic Geographic Area	Productivity per Laborer in Dollars		
	Primary Sector	Secondary Sector	Tertiary Sector
North America	2,860	5,530	5,200
Oceania	4,150	2,360	2,430
Northwest Europe	1,040	1,700	1,590
Southeast Europe	310	1,280	720
Latin America	360	1,120	1,480
Japan	400	1,100	1,020
Near East	280	690	680
Southeast Asia	170	370	380

development.[7] But Table 3.4 certainly does not show that the lower the per capita income the greater the difference between income in the primary and secondary sector. We are much more inclined to think that the ratio remains rather constant over time. Figure 3.1, for instance, shows how the ratio changed in the past forty years in the United States.[8] Although during the period 1910-56 huge cyclical fluctuations in the ratio took place, no trend—neither positive nor negative—can be observed. One might argue that these data on the U.S.

Table 3.4

PRODUCTION PER LABORER IN THE PRIMARY AND
TERTIARY SECTORS, AS PERCENTAGE OF THE
SECONDARY SECTOR

Economic Geographic Area	Primary Sector	Tertiary Sector
North America	54	97
Northwest Europe	62	94
Southeast Europe	24	56
Latin America	33	132
Japan	33	92
Near East	41	99
Southeast Asia	40	101

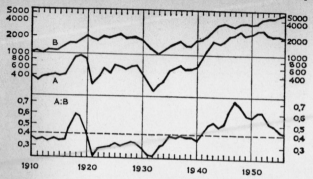

FIG. 3.1   Ratio between per capita income in agriculture (A) and in other sectors (B) in the United States, 1910-56

income ratios do not give us much information about the situation in poor countries. However, the ratios in the United States can be traced back over a period of 140 years, using wage data for earlier years. For England we could go back even to the fourteenth century, using wage data published by Steffen, and for Japan good basic material was available back to 1880.

The ratios in all countries show a remarkable stability, but even more noteworthy is the fact that they differ so little between the various countries: during the period 1880-1930 the ratio was 0.43 in England, 0.40 in the United States, and 0.38 in Japan.[9]

A glance at the older English data demonstrates that in earlier times the ratio deteriorated detrimentally to agriculture. We think therefore that we are not far from the truth by assuming that originally income differentials between the agrarian sector and the others were very small.[10] As far as England is concerned we therefore come to the conclusion that the deterioration set in with industrialization; but Japan shows for the period 1880-1920 a definite improvement. One gets the impression that at the point where agrarian income is about 40 per cent of that in the other sectors a kind of

Table 3.5

PER CAPITA INCOME IN THE PRIMARY SECTOR AS
PERCENTAGE OF THE PER CAPITA INCOME IN
THE OTHER SECTORS*

Period	England	United States	Japan
1301-1400	79		
1401-1500	70		
1501-1600	66		
1601-1700	69		
1701-1800	50		
1801-1810	52		
1811-1820	53		
1821-1830	34	34	
1831-1840	44	35	
1841-1850	43	36	
1851-1860	44	37	
1861-1870	48	39	
1871-1880	43	37	
1881-1890	43	37	33
1891-1900	42	45	39
1901-1910	43	46	40
1911-1920	44	42	42
1921-1930	44	29	35
1931-1940	49	33	26
1941-1950	71	55	—
1951-1960	76	49	37

* Computed from G. F. Steffen, *Studien zur Geschichte der
Englischen Lohnarbeiter* (1905), Vols. I, II, III; A. L. Bowley,
Wages and Income in the United Kingdom since 1860 (1937);
A. L. Bowley, *Wages, Earnings and Hours of Work, 1914-1947*
(1947); J. R. Bellerby, *Agriculture and Industry* (1956), and
an unpublished paper by W. L. Posthumus; K. Okkawa, *The
Growth Rate of the Japanese Economy* (1957).

status quo sets in. But this also means that the long-term
increase in labor productivity in agriculture and industry were about equal. However the increase in productivity should have been much greater in agriculture than
in industry in order to permit agriculture to catch up
with the other sectors.

When agricultural employment becomes relatively
unimportant the Government is always in a position to

improve agrarian earnings through subsidies and other forms of income transfer. Such a policy is strongly supported by agrarian pressure groups. However, one might discuss if a further decrease in agrarian employment would not be more advantageous for the country as a whole.

It appears somewhat puzzling that labor has continued to stay such a long time in agriculture although income in other activities is so much higher. We will see later that in low-income countries this is indeed partly due to the fact that no other employment possibilities exist. But apart from this, one should realize that whereas industrial labor is paid according to its *marginal productivity,* the members of the agrarian family in the traditional agrarian society receive the *average product* of their labor. Figure 3.2 gives a somewhat

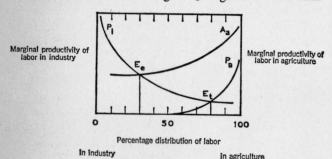

FIG. 3.2   Equilibrium between remuneration in the industrial and agrarian sector

exaggerated picture of such a situation. If we assume a given amount of capital in industry, and a given quantity of arable land, marginal productivity of labor in one of the sectors will fall if more labor is added to that sector. If in both sectors income were to be determined by marginal productivity, labor would distribute itself over the two sectors in such a way that, in the equilibrium situation, the marginal products in both sectors (P_i and P_a) would be equal (assuming complete mobility of labor and complete rational economic behavior). In our example this would be the case in E_t, and it would mean that about 20 per cent of labor would be employed in agriculture and 80 per cent in industry. However, if the members of the agrarian (joint) family receive the average product of labor, P_a would no longer indicate the supply of agrarian labor but A_a. In our example, this would mean that about 70 per cent would be employed in agriculture, although marginal agrarian productivity has already fallen to zero a long time ago. But then income per laborer is of course much lower in agriculture than in industry. In spite of this interpretation we have to admit that we consider the great stability over time, together with the great uniformity in various countries, of the income ratio of agrarian and nonagrarian as a phenomenon still not yet fully explained.

So far we have compared the income relation between the primary and the other sectors. We may also compare the incomes earned in the three sectors in the various economic-geographic areas with those received in the richest ones—i.e., in North America. Some are given in Table 3.6. We can draw from this table a few

Table 3.6

PRODUCTION PER LABORER IN THE PRIMARY,
SECONDARY, AND TERTIARY SECTORS IN VARIOUS
ECONOMIC-GEOGRAPHIC AREAS AS PERCENTAGES OF
THE PRODUCTION IN THE SAME SECTORS IN
NORTH AMERICA (ABOUT 1953)

Economic-Geographic Area	Primary Sector	Secondary Sector	Tertiary Sector
North America	100	100	100
Northwest Europe	36	32	31
Southeast Europe	11	24	15
Latin America	13	21	28
Japan	14	20	20
Near East	10	11	13
Southeast Asia	6	7	7

interesting conclusions. We see that in Northwest Europe, the Near East and in Southeast Asia practically the same relationship exists between the production in the primary and in the other sectors as in North America. That is, in *all the three sectors* the production per laborer was in Northwest Europe about one-third of that in North America, against one-tenth in the Near East and one-fourteenth in South East Asia.

In the other areas the situation is less clear. One gets the impression that in Southeast Europe, in Latin America, and in Japan the productivity in the secondary sector, as compared with North America, is about twice as high as in the primary sector. It is not impossible that these discrepancies will disappear during the process of industrialization. But the statement in the U.N. Report that this would be a general tendency does not find a confirmation in the other data.

We can recapitulate our findings as follows:

(*a*) All over the world per capita production in agriculture is considerably lower than in the secondary and tertiary sectors; per capita income in the secondary and tertiary sectors tends to be equal;

(*b*) In countries with a low per capita income, income is low in *all* three sectors and in some cases it is lower in the same proportion;

(*c*) In all low-income countries percentage employment in the primary sector is considerably higher than in the rich countries.

Thus two factors play a role in the explanation of low per capita incomes: first, the percentage distribution of labor over the three sectors, and second the labor productivity in the sectors. Table 3.7 demonstrates this for a few economic-geographic areas (the figures are somewhat rounded off). We thus see that in all areas per capita income in the primary sector is lower than in the others, and that in the poorer areas a far greater per-

Table 3.7

COMPONENTS OF PER CAPITA INCOME DIFFERENTIALS
(ABOUT 1953)

1	2	3	4	5	6	7
Economic Geographic Area	Percentage Employment in Primary Sector	Per Capita Income in Primary Sector	Percentage Employment in Other Sectors	Per Capita Income in Other Sectors	Per Capita Income = $(2 \times 3) + (4 \times 5):100$	Index of Per Capita Income
Northwest Europe	20	380	80	760	680	100
Latin America	50	130	50	390	260	40
Near East	70	90	30	225	130	20
Far East	80	55	20	120	68	10

centage employment is concentrated in the sector with the lowest productivity than in the richer ones.

PER CAPITA INCOME AND ENERGY CONSUMPTION

Because per capita income is correlated with percentage employment in nonagrarian activities and because an increase in industrial production asks for more energy consumption, we may assume the existence of a correlation between per capita income and energy consumption. The relation has been examined already in an E.C.L.A. publication,[11] where the correlation between per capita consumption of electricity in manufacturing and mining M and gross domestic product per capita P was computed. The following equation was found:

$$\log M = 1.2683 \log P - 0.1566$$
$$(R = 0.90)$$

We computed the correlation between per capita income and per capita energy consumption (coal equivalent) for 30 countries (see Table 3.8) and developed the following equation:

$$\log y = 1.4572 \log x - 0.8239$$
$$(R = 0.95)$$

where y is the per capita income and x the per capita energy consumption. The correlation is rather high, and we derived from the equation the "theoretical" energy consumption at a \$200 and \$800 per capita income level, namely 340 and 2,550 kg.

CONSUMPTION ITEMS AND
SOCIAL CONDITIONS

Thus far we have dealt with inputs in the economic process only. The percentage distribution of employment indicates the division of labor inputs over the three sectors of the economy, and energy consumption shows

Table 3.8

PER CAPITA INCOME, ENERGY CONSUMPTION,
NEWSPRINT AND MOTORCARS (ABOUT 1959)

	Country	Per Capita Income in 1953 Dollars	Energy Consumption, Coal Equivalent, kg	Newsprint Consumption, kg	Motorcars per 10,000 Inhabitants
1	United States	$1,940	7,830	36.1	3,350
2	Canada	1,320	5,600	24.1	2,180
3	Switzerland	1,250	1,670	14.1	860
4	Sweden	1,130	3,000	26.0	1,460
5	Belgium	900	3,850	11.7	760
6	United Kingdom	880	4,600	22.1	960
7	France	880	2,370	10.6	1,110
8	Norway	830	2,480	13.9	540
9	Germany	700	3,270	8.6	670
10	Finland	660	1,400	17.2	370
11	Czechoslovakia	630	—	1.8	—
12	Netherlands	590	2,670	12.2	400
13	Poland	580	—	1.9	360
14	Puerto Rico	540	1,140	5.1	490
15	Austria	520	1,960	11.2	480
16	Ireland	440	1,340	11.6	560
17	Italy	410	920	4.9	340
18	Argentina	390	1,030	6.5	200
19	Hungary	380	—	3.4	—
20	Chile	330	790	2.9	80
21	Spain	310	830	2.2	80
22	Bulgaria	290	—	3.2	—
23	Rumania	280	—	1.9	—
24	Yugoslavia	280	800	1.7	20
25	Japan	270	970	7.3	30
26	Colombia	260	470	1.6	60
27	Mexico	230	820	2.4	130
28	Guatemala	230	160	1.0	50
29	Portugal	210	360	2.6	160
30	Philippines	170	150	1.5	30
31	Ceylon	120	100	1.0	80
32	Thailand	80	70	0.9	16
33	India	70	150	0.2	16
34	Pakistan	70	60	0.1	6
35	Burma	60	50	0.5	9

the power intake in the production process.* But when inputs increase, income goes up and so does consumption, because consumption is a function of income. Already in the last century E. Engel, the German statistician from Saxon, found his famous law according to which the percentage of income spent on food decreases when income goes up. Much has been written in the last decade on the relationship between per capita income and food consumption measured in calories and proteins. Although the topic is rather controversial, we can state with certainty that in the poorest part of the world food consumption is insufficient. It seems precarious, however, to correlate food consumption in various countries with per capita income only. The results were in any case not convincing.

Much better results were obtained with a few other consumption items, where the interrelation is undisputable. First of all we computed the correlation between per capita income and the number of motorcars.† Due to car registration, introduced in all countries, it is easy to find exact statistical data for this purpose. We developed the following equation:

$$\log y = 1.7692 \log x - 2.2431$$
$$(R = 0.94)$$

where y is the per capita income and x the number of motor cars per 10,000 inhabitants. For the $200 and $800 level we computed 70 and 780 motor cars per 10,000 inhabitants.

Next we developed the correlation between per capita income and newsprint consumption (in kg) per capita. This relationship seems of particular interest because an international comparison of literacy and education is rather arbitrary, due to the deficiency of the statistical data. Newsprint consumption, then, indicates

---

* However, private consumption is included in our data; we assumed, therefore, that industrial and private consumption change in the same proportion.

† Not trucks, because they are means of production.

in any case how people practice their reading ability. The following equation was established:

$$\log y = 1.396 \log x - 2.9976$$
$$(R = 0.89)$$

where y is the per capita income and x the newsprint consumption per capita. Because the correlation coefficient was lower than those found so far, a second glance at the figures used showed immediately that the data of the communist countries* did not fit into the picture. They are all considerably lower than the figures of other countries with equal per capita income. This may be partly due to the fact that advertising is not yet allowed in communist countries. This might explain the low figures for Hungary, Bulgaria, Rumania, and Yugoslavia,† but certainly not those of Czechoslovakia and Poland. The only explanation then must be that the governments in those countries do not give a high priority to newsprint.

Exclusion of the communist countries gave the following equation:

$$\log y = 1.4454 \log x - 3.0718$$
$$(R = 0.93)$$

where again y is the per capita income and x the per capita newsprint consumption.

The correlation coefficient increased considerably (from 0.8950 to 0.9335),‡ but the elasticity coefficient (1.396 and 1.445) and the constant term remained practically unchanged. But from these two equations we may learn something more. Without doubt many varia-

* The *Statistical Yearbook of the United Nations* does not publish data on energy consumption and motor cars for the communist countries.

† As a first approximation it is assumed that advertisements use about half of the newspaper space.

‡ From a statistical point of view, our figures on newsprint consumption, motor cars, and energy consumption have a much greater accuracy than the national income data. The good correlations we found *in all three cases* with the income data have certainly increased our confidence in our income estimates.

bles of the social system will change together with per capita income. However the social and economic policy of the government and specific factor endowments of the various countries may cause significant deviations. Therefore we think that further study in the divergences of the regression lines are certainly needed in order to understand the particularities of the individual countries. But our high correlations indicate that those deviations are, generally speaking, smaller than one would expect.

Because per capita newsprint consumption might be considered as a rough indicator of the degree of education in a country, the relation discussed in the preceding section gives at the same time some insight into existing correlations between per capita income and social conditions. One of the social conditions directly related to economics is the length of the work week. For U.S. time series, Verdoorn[12] computed the correlation between labor productivity in industry and hours of work per week. After adding the data for 1950 we again com-

Table 3.9

LABOR PRODUCTIVITY AND HOURS OF WORK
PER WEEK IN U.S. INDUSTRY

Year	Index of Labor Productivity	Hours of Work per Week
1850	100	71.0
1860	152	66.6
1870	151	63.4
1880	176	61.1
1890	253	58.1
1900	298	56.1
1910	311	54.8
1920	346	50.8
1930	537	48.7
1940	711	40.2
1950	857	40.5

puted the correlation. We found the following equation:

$$\log p = -0.3580 \log h + 8.6811$$
$$(R = -0.982)$$

where p is the index of labor productivity and h the hours of work per week. The correlation is much higher than anything one can expect with an international comparison in this field. A great many countries have adopted the eight-hour working day, but some doubt may arise whether the official figures—published in the *I.L.O. Statistical Yearbooks*—always give a realistic picture of the actual working hours in all countries. On the other hand, several low-income countries show very short working weeks, but this could be due to existing surplus capacity and great unemployment. We selected

Table 3.10

PER CAPITA INCOME AND LENGTH OF THE
WORKING WEEK, 1960

Country	Per Capita Income, 1952-54 Dollars	Length of the Working Week
1. United States	$1,940	39.7
2. Canada	1,320	40.4
3. Czechoslovakia	630	41.4
4. Norway	830	42.9
5. Austria	520	43.5
6. France	880	45.5
7. West Germany	700	45.6
8. United Kingdom	880	46.1
9. Netherlands	590	48.9
10. Colombia	260	50.0
11. Japan	270	50.6

a few countries that made a rather reasonable impression* and found the following equation:

$$\log y = -0.5815 \log x + 12.4398$$
$$(R = -0.897)$$

* Compare Table 3.8 in which *all* available figures are collected; unfortunately working hours data are available only for a much smaller group of countries, and in a few cases they really made no sense.

where *y* is per capita income and *x* the length of the
work week. Although the correlation coefficient is not
too high, we think that our "theoretical" values at the
$200 and $800 income level—i.e., 55.4 and 43.5 hours
per week—are not unreasonable. But we must add here
that the official statistics from countries with per capita
incomes of about $200 indicate much shorter working
weeks.

The "demonstration effect" [13] seems to have had such
an influence in low-income countries that they all have
adopted at least an eight-hour working day. The question arises however, how far such legislation is en-
forced. Further, one might ask if at those low wage
levels the laborers would not be better off with longer
working hours and higher wages.

Many social scientists have drawn attention to the
existence of a correlation between per capita income
and sanitary conditions as measured, for example, by
the number of hospital beds per 1,000 inhabitants, or
the number of doctors per 10,000 inhabitants.

R. Olivier[14] has brought some material[15] together in
order to prove this thesis. He has plotted the data in
graphs (compare Fig. 3.3) and has drawn freehand(?)
regression lines. The graph clearly demonstrates that
the low-income countries, on the average, have much
inferior sanitary conditions than the richer ones, but the
correlation coefficients we computed turned out to be
very low ($R = 0.476$ for hospital beds and 0.790 for
doctors). These results are not surprising because the
graphs show important dispersions along the regression
lines.

Therefore we can only give some tentative estimates
for the sanitary conditions at the $200 and $800 income
level—namely, 40 and 90 hospital beds per 1,000 inhabitants and 40 and 100 doctors per 100,000 inhabitants. But it is especially in this field that various
countries show their own peculiarities, and their own
idiosyncrasies.

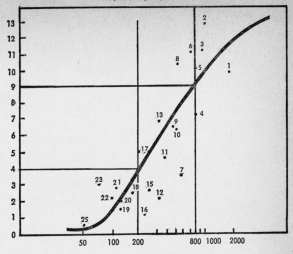

Hospital beds per 1,000 inhabitants

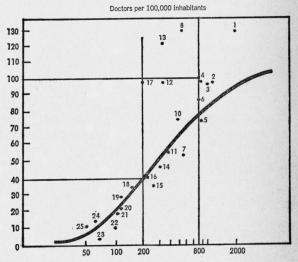

Doctors per 100,000 inhabitants

1. U.S.A.; 2. Switzerland; 3. Australia; 4. Belgium; 5. U.K.; 6. France; 7. Venezuela; 8. W. Germany; 9. Israel; 10. Argentina; 11. Chile; 12. Cuba; 13. Italy; 14. Union of South Africa; 15. Colombia; 16. Mexico; 17. Japan; 18. Dominican Republic; 19. Egypt; 20. Peru; 21. Ceylon; 22. Rhodesia and Nyasaland; 23. Belgian Congo; 24. India; 25. Burma.

FIG. 3.3 Per capita income and sanitary conditions

TAXATION

A completely different field in which fundamental differences between rich and poor countries are to be found is taxation. First of all it has been observed[16] that rich countries have a much higher taxation as a percentage of national income than low income countries. The following table has been taken from the Annual Report of the Kreditanstalt für Wiederaufbau, 1962:

Table 3.11

TOTAL TAXATION AS A PERCENTAGE OF NATIONAL INCOME (1960)

Country	Per Capita Income, 1960 Dollars	Taxation as a Percentage of National Income
North America	$2,500	27
Common Market and E.F.T.A.ª	1,110	30
Oceania, Japan, South Africa	510	21
Finland, Greece, Eire, Iceland, Spain, Yugoslavia, Malta, Portugal, Turkey, Cyprus	340	13
Near East	310	19
Central America	270	8
South America	250	11
Africa North of Sahara	180	14
Far East	100	14
Africa South of Sahara	80	11
Southeast Asia	70	10

ª Without Portugal.

The correlation is not very high ($R = 0.82$) but the values we found for the $200 and $800 income levels, i.e., 13 per cent and 24 per cent, fit well into the general picture (compare Table 3.11). Strangely enough, the social and economic policies followed in the various countries seem to have had but a minor influence on the percentage. We are inclined to believe that the richer the country, the more it has to administer and hence the higher (relatively speaking, of course) its taxation.

But this does not mean that politics have no influence whatsoever on taxation in a country. However, it is fairly evident that political pressure is of much greater importance as far as the *distribution* between direct and indirect taxes, than as far as taxation as a percentage of national income is concerned. We may state as a general rule that the lower the per capita income the higher the percentage of indirect tax in total tax revenue. This phenomenon cannot only be observed when we compare rich and poor countries, but also countries that are rich today show in time series the same tendency. For example, the United Kingdom had in the period 1840-1850 a per capita income of about $200 (in 1952-54 prices), and the direct taxes were about 27 per cent of the total revenue; Colombia's per capita income amounted over the period 1948-55 also to about $200, and direct taxes were 26 per cent of the total tax revenue.

In most of the poor countries (as in the United Kingdom in the beginning of the past century) the ruling groups do their utmost to have the taxes paid by the poor.* If, as certainly happened in the United Kingdom at that time, an important amount of the incomes of the higher-income brackets is plowed back into industry, the policy might even be defended with the simple wage-fund argument of classical economists. According to the wage-fund theory, additional employment asks for savings, and because savings are furnished by the higher incomes, an income tax will increase savings and hence employment. Unfortunately in many of the poor countries the rich people do not use their incomes to increase employment—in any case not in their own country. But in spite of this fact, most of their politicians seem to be excellent disciples of the wage-fund theory.

With the increase in political power of the lower income groups—and in Western Europe this went hand in

* And by foreign companies, of course.

hand with the increase in per capita income—a shift in the tax structure toward direct taxation set in.

Simone Clemhout[17] computed long-term series for the United Kingdom and Sweden, which show this tendency clearly (Table 3.12). She also compared the per capita

Table 3.12

PER CAPITA INCOME AND DIRECT TAXES AS A
PERCENTAGE OF TAX REVENUE

	United Kingdom		Sweden	
Year	Per Capita Income, 1952-54 Dollars	Direct Taxes as a Percentage of Total Tax Revenue (Trend Values)	Per Capita Income, 1929 Kr	Direct Taxes as a Percentage of Total Tax Revenue (Trend Values)
1800	110	23		
1812	110	23		
1820	150	24		
1840	180	26		
1850	240	28		
1860	260	30	395	17
1870	260	32	470	16
1880	310	35	560	16
1890	390	37	640	17
1900	450	40	840	19
1910	480	43	1,060	22
1920	480	46	1,360	25
1930	550	50	1,570	28
1940	680	54	1,860	33
1950	720	58	2,670	37

income data of sixteen countries with the percentage of direct taxes of total tax revenue. The correlation turned out to be satisfactory ($R = 0.89$), but was considerably better when the direct taxes as a percentage of total tax revenue were correlated with newsprint consumption per capita ($R = 0.96$).

We have already indicated that although per capita income is a good comprehensive indicator of the level of living, some other indicators can be used as well. Because the correlation between per capita income and per

Table 3.13

PER CAPITA INCOME, NEWSPRINT CONSUMPTION
PER CAPITA AND DIRECT TAXES AS A PERCENTAGE
OF TOTAL TAX REVENUE (1948-55)

Country	Average Per Capita Income, 1948-55 Dollars	Per Capita newsprint consumption in kg, 1948-55	Direct Taxes as a Percentage of Total Tax Revenue
1. United States	$1,730	31.5	87.7
2. Canada	1,200	19.4	54.0
3. Sweden	1,040	18.4	48.5
4. New Zealand	960	15.0	68.5
5. Belgium	810	9.0	41.5
6. United Kingdom	740	9.8	49.8
7. France	650	8.8	41.9
8. Netherlands	500	5.6	47.1
9. Chile	370	4.2	31.1
10. Brazil	240	1.6	31.5
11. Costa Rica	230	1.8	19.6
12. Colombia	220	1.3	25.7
13. Mexico	190	2.2	22.9
14. Egypt	130	0.6	20.3
15. Ceylon	120	1.2	25.0
16. Nigeria	80		17.7

capita newsprint consumption is high ($R = 0.93$), it goes without saying that newsprint consumption may be also used for this purpose. In this case, however, the correlation with newsprint consumption might be of special interest, if we assume that these data might not only be considered as an indicator of the level of literacy in a country, but also as an indicator of the political activity of the mass of the population. Because political activity of the low-income groups in a country seems to be a precondition for a change of a highly undemocratic tax structure where the low incomes bear, through indirect taxes, the main burden of taxation, the high correlation with per capita newsprint consumption is rather interesting.

It would have been better still if political scientists

could have furnished us with an index of political activity in the various countries. Then we would have tried to "explain" the differences in the tax structure with two variables: per capita income and a political index. Unfortunately political science is still in its infancy so far as the quantification of its most important variables is concerned, and therefore this was impossible. But because the correlation with per capita income only was fairly close, it seems permissible to compute the percentages for the $200 and the $800 income level, namely 23 per cent and 55 per cent.

A STRUCTURAL TOPOGRAPHY OF RICH AND POOR COUNTRIES

Table 3.14 gives the results of our finding in a concise form. The numerical values of the various correlation coefficients in the table are high enough to demonstrate that our approach to economic growth and progress in terms of changes in per capita income has operational significance.

Table 3.14
PER CAPITA INCOME AND SOME STRUCTURAL DATA

Item	$200	$800	R
1. Percentage employment in the secondary and tertiary sector	48	78	0.92
2. Energy consumption per capita (coal equivalent, kg)	340	2,550	0.95
3. Motor cars per 10,000 inhabitants	70	780	0.94
4. Newsprint consumption per capita, kg	1.8	13.3	0.89
5. Working hours per week	55	43	0.90
6. Hospital beds per 1,000 inhabitants[a]	4	9	—
7. Doctors per 100,000 inhabitants[a]	40	100	—
8. Taxation as percentage of national income	13	24	0.82
9. Direct taxes as percentage of total tax revenue	23	55	0.89

[a] Estimated, not computed.

Because the correlations are sufficiently high, we have brought all the regression lines together in Figs. 3.4(*a*) and 3.4(*b*).

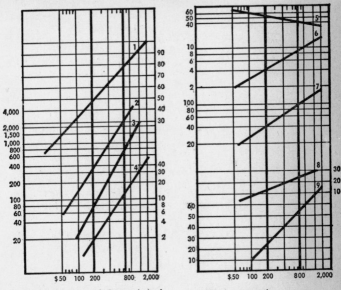

1. Percentage employment in the secondary and tertiary sector
2. Energy consumption per capita (coal equivalent, kg)
3. Motor cars per 10,000 inhabitants
4. Newsprint consumption per capita, kg

5. Working hours per week
6. Hospital beds per 1,000 inhabitants
7. Doctors per 100,000 inhabitants
8. Taxation as percentage of national income
9. Direct taxes as percentage of total tax revenue

FIGS. 3.4a and 3.4b   Structural topography of rich and poor countries

For explanation, see Table 3.14.

These graphs may be considered as a first attempt to a structural topography of rich and poor countries. If the per capita income of an area is known, it is easy to find in the graphs the numerical values of the various variables. In those cases where the correlation coefficients were high, deviations from the computed values are likely to be small. But even when the correlations were not too good, the data may be of some use as first approximations.

We think that the data are also of a certain interest for planning purposes, because they clearly demonstrate the interrelationship between per capita income and other data. We do not intend to suggest that a government designing the development of a country has to follow the paths of our regression lines, but perhaps they might be considered as long-term equilibria.

NOTES

1. Compare J. Tinbergen, "Quelques problèmes posés par le concept de structure économique," *Revue d'Economie Politique,* January 1952, p. 28.

2. S. S. Kuznets, "International Differences in Income Levels," in *Economic Change, Selected Essays* (1953).

3. B. Singh, *Population and Food Planning in India* (1957), p. 62.

4. See K. Mandelbaum, *The Industrialization of Backward Areas* (1955), p. 4.

5. Computed for the year 1953 by V. Escala in an unpublished paper, Institute of Social Studies; for 1957 similar computations have been made by A. K. Atallah. The outcomes were practically the same.

6. Compare M. S. Khan, *India's Economic Development and International Economic Relations* (1961), p. 81.

7. *Analysis and Projection of Economic Development,* United Nations (1955), p. 15.

8. Computation by W. L. Posthumus, unpublished paper, Institute of Social Studies.

9. These ratios of course do not tell us anything about the absolute levels in the various countries.

10. One has to take into consideration that, due to the high costs of transportation, food was much cheaper in the countryside than in the towns, and the poor spend about 80 per cent of their income on food. (Compare T. D. Black, "Agriculture in the Nation's Economy," *American Economic Review,* 1956.)

11. Economic Commission for Latin America, "Situation Actual y Evolucion Reciente de la Industria de la Energia

Electrica en America Latina," Santiago, 1961 (mimeographed).

12. Our data, except those for 1950, are taken from P. J. Verdoorn, *Arbeidsduur en welvaartspeil* (1947), p. 44.

13. Compare R. Nurkse, *Problems of Capital Formation in Underdeveloped Countries* (1955), p. 58.

14. R. Olivier, *Planification en Afrique* (Paris: Ministère de la Coopération, Centre de Documentation, 1963), Vol. II, p. 213.

15. From the *Demographic Yearbooks of the United Nations*.

16. See *Jahresbericht, XIV,* Kreditanstalt für Wiederaufbau, Frankfurt (1962), p. 25.

17. In an unpublished paper, Institute of Social Studies, The Hague.

Chapter 4

ECONOMIC GROWTH

We indicated in Chapter I that we speak of economic growth when the long-term percentage increase in total output Y equals the long term percentage increase in population P, thus if

$$\frac{\Delta Y}{Y} = \frac{\Delta P}{P}$$

If we assume a fixed relation between population and the total labor force L—in other words, between the total economically active population on the one hand, and total population on the other[1]—economic growth can also be represented as a situation where

$$\frac{\Delta Y}{Y} = \frac{\Delta L}{L}$$

Some reflection will make clear that it was exactly this problem of economic growth that puzzled classical economists. They observed a rapid increase in population and their problem was under which conditions it would be possible for the economy to produce enough (food) to sustain the rapidly increasing population—in other words, to keep per capita output constant and equal to the subsistence level.

A long-term increase in per capita income was thought to be impossible, due to the combination of the Malthusian law of population and the law of diminishing returns working on the scarce agent of production—land.

In our solution of this problem we follow the Harrod-Domar model.[2] We further assume, as did the classical economists, that technology will remain constant; but unlike Ricardo and Stuart Mill we assume that the supply of labor (being a fixed proportion of the population) is not affected by the wage level. In other words, we assume that the labor supply is completely inelastic in relation to per capita income.

THE HARROD-DOMAR MODEL

We start from Keynes's simple definition of national income:

$$Y = C + I \qquad (1)$$

where C = total consumption and I = total net investment. Because consumption depends on income, we may write

$$C = cY \qquad (2)$$

where c = the average rate of consumption.

Further we assume a fixed relationship between the increase in capital ($\Delta K = I$) and the increase in income (ΔY)

$$\frac{\Delta K}{\Delta Y} = k$$

where k thus equals the capital coefficient (capital output ratio). But this can also be written in the form

$$I = \Delta K = k \, \Delta Y \qquad (3)$$

If we combine Eqs. (2) and (3) in Eq. (1) we get

$$Y = cY + k \, \Delta Y$$

or

$$Y - cY = k \, \Delta Y$$
$$(1 - c) \, Y = k \, \Delta Y$$

But because $(1 - c)$ is the average rate of saving, we may write

$$sY = k \, \Delta Y$$

From which it follows that

$$\frac{\Delta Y}{Y} = \frac{s}{k}$$

Thus under growth conditions

$$\frac{\Delta L}{L} = \frac{s}{k}$$

And because we assumed a constant relationship between the labor force and the population, we may also write

$$p = \frac{s}{k}$$

where p is the percentage increase in population. That is, so long as the ratio between the average rate of savings and the capital coefficient equals the percentage increase in population, the per capita income remains constant. If we indicate by $\dot{y}$ the percentage increase in per capita income, then we find that

$$\dot{y} = \frac{s}{k} - p$$

Given the rate of population increase p and the technology k, it is the rate of savings (investments) that will determine the amount of additional labor that can be absorbed in the economic process. If

$$p > \frac{s}{k}.$$

it will not be possible to employ all the additional labor force, and part of it will become unemployed or disguised unemployed.* This means that according to this theoretical approach it is a feature of the growth economy, that once a special technique is given, labor and

---

* Disguised unemployed are those people, who, although engaged in one way or another in the process of production, do not add anything to the total output—viz., their marginal productivity is equal to zero, or sometimes even negative.

capital are completely complementary—i.e., no substitution between the factors of production is possible. We think that this assumption is rather realistic; it explains in any case the huge disguised unemployment in the primary and tertiary sector, observed in so many of the poor countries, where p is rather high and saving ($= \Delta K$) is rather small. We can easily demonstrate this interrelationship in a graph.[3] In Fig. 4.1, L is the total labor force and g the slope of the g function, is the percentage growth of the labor force.

The g function is supposed to be an independent variable. As L indicates the total labor force and Y the total output, the slope of the y function indicates the relationship between output and labor. In order to employ more labor additional investment ($\Delta K = I$) has to be undertaken and the slope of the k function indicates the investment needed for additional employment (the so-called capital intensity, K/L). But those investments have to be financed out of savings and the slope of the

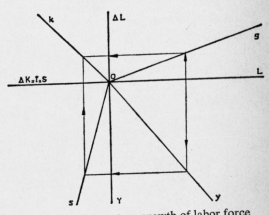

FIG. 4.1   Percentage growth of labor force

s function—the second independent variable—indicates the savings out of current production. Because under growth conditions

$$\frac{\Delta Y/Y}{\Delta L/L} = 1$$

this growth situation is represented by the y function, which, starting in the origin of LOY, has a slope of $-\dfrac{gk}{s}$.

In order to keep Y/L constant over time there exists, given the slope of the g function (the increase in population) and given the slope of the k function (the technology), only one numerical value of the average rate of savings that guarantees a constant per capita output (or what is the same a constant productivity of labor). There exists, under the given assumptions, only one level of investment that allows the absorption of the additional labor force in the process of production without a change in the average output. A lower level of investment will inevitably lead to unemployment, whether or not disguised.

This can also be easily demonstrated in a graph. In Fig. 4.2 the slope of the k function has the same mean-

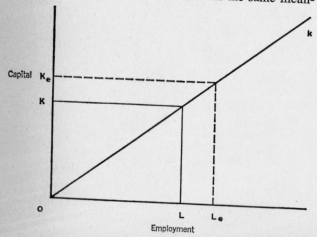

FIG. 4.2   Capital stock versus employment

ing as in Fig. 4.1. Given a certain capital stock *OK*, the amount of employment is determined: *OL*. If the labor force would be, however, *OL_e*, then *LL_e* is either unemployed or disguised unemployed. The only possibility to employ *LL_e* is to increase the capital stock with *KK_e*: it requires, in other words, an investment equal to *KK_e*.

One might ask if a theory of economic growth built on our rather rigid assumptions can be considered as realistic.

According to P. C. Mahalanobis,[5] we may assume for India that $p = 1.25$, $s = 5$ and $k = 3.3$, in any case for the period prior to 1952. Applying the formula

$$\dot{y} = \frac{s}{k} - p$$

we find

$$0.25 = \frac{5}{3.3} - 1.25$$

which means that the long-term percentage increase in per capita income in India has been about 0.25 per cent per annum, against the 0.38 per cent we found over the period 1860-1960 (see p. 41). This means practically *no* increase in per capita income. If we assume a rate of savings that is a trifle lower ($s = 4.9$) and both an increase in population and a capital-output ratio a little higher ($p = 1.4$ and $k = 3.5$ respectively), we arrive at the long-term growth situation:

$$0 = \frac{4.9}{3.5} - 1.4$$

However, Mahalanobis's figures demonstrate that our simple growth model can be used to understand what has actually happened in Southeast Asia over a rather long period. We assume that the same might be said for the Middle East and for Central Africa, but with the exception of Egypt no statistical data are available to prove this thesis.

The foregoing analysis more or less forces us to conclude that the only way to break through the Malthusian low-per-capita-income equilibrium of the growth situation is by way of a huge shift in the rate of investment —in saving or in capital imports. For in order to realize an annual 2 per cent increase in per capita income under the conditions of the Mahalanobis model, we would need a rate of savings of

$$2 + 1.25 = \frac{s}{3.3}$$
$$s = 10.6$$

Therefore, if Rostow says that a rise is needed in the rate of investment from, say, 5 per cent of the national income to 10 per cent or more in order to realize a take-off into self-sustained growth,[6] his statement is not much more than a truism so long as one thinks in terms of the Harrod-Domar model.

Along the same line of thought one comes to the theory of the vicious circle of low-income countries: because income is low, savings are low, capital formation is small, productivity remains low and income remains low.[7]

Further, the theory gives the theoretical foundation of international financial aid. For if the poor countries are so poor that they cannot save enough to increase their national incomes to a desirable level, aid from the richer countries seems the only way out. Because we have to criticize practically all the assumptions of the Harrod-Domar model in the following paragraphs, we should like to state in advance that we are very much in favor of international aid; we even think it could be still considerably higher. But we also think that it is very dangerous for the poor countries themselves when they assume that only through *foreign* assistance can their problems be solved.

THE CAPITAL COEFFICIENT AND LABOR PRODUCTIVITY

In his chapter "Inadequacy of Economic Theories of Growth," E. E. Hagen strongly attacks the idea that the poor countries are too poor to save enough to finance economic development. He quotes W. A. Lewis: ". . . Least of all can those nations plead poverty as an excuse for not saving in which 40 per cent or so of the national income is squandered by the top 10 per cent of income receivers, living luxuriously on rents." [8] Reduction by one fourth in the level of consumption of those high-income families would provide resources ample for sufficient investment for economic growth.[9]

Unfortunately, it is impossible to know how much the top income brackets in many poor countries actually do save,* but one has the impression that they probably save quite a bit—not at home but abroad. Having a numbered bank account in Switzerland seems even to be a status symbol in many poor countries. Although we can blame the rich for not investing enough at home,† let us not forget that their attitude is completely rational in those countries where the political situation is unstable. In countries where no rich man knows what will happen to him or to his property the next year, a numbered bank account in Switzerland makes a lot of sense.

But more important seems the argument that in none of the poor (i.e., the largely agrarian) countries, are the rich people (i.e., the landlords) in favor of economic development. Economic development will in the long run inevitably lead to an increase in the demand for (industrial) labor, hence to a decrease in (disguised) unemployment and to an increase in the wage rate. In the

---

* I am afraid that Hagen and Lewis do not know this either.
† And also for the normal way in which they invest at home.

long run, it will also, as a result of this, increase the
land-man ratio and thus decrease the rent of land. Add
to this fact that (direct) taxation increases when per
capita income goes up, and one has enough arguments
to understand that rich landlords are not in favor of industrialization. One can, of course, blame them for being
shortsighted, but let us not forget that England and
Japan "took off" without the aid of the big landlords. In
Hagen's tables of the social origin of England's and
Japan's social leaders[10] during the period of economic
development, there is only a small percentage of landlords.

Thus, although it is possible to say from a purely economic point of view that investment could be higher in
low-income countries, this statement does not mean
much as soon as we consider the sociological, political,
and psychological aspects of the problem.

We certainly do not offer the foregoing criticism in
order to demonstrate that, because we cannot expect the
highest income brackets in the poor countries to invest
considerably more at home than they have done thus far,
savings and investment cannot go up considerably in the
low-income countries. We do not think that countries
cannot save because they are poor. We believe that the
whole idea that saving means an *absolute* decrease in
the level of consumption is wrong. It is not the *average*
but the *marginal* rate of savings that counts. Although
it is true that in poor countries the average rate of savings is low because the greatest part of the population is
living near to the subsistence level, this does not mean
that the marginal rate has to be low also. On the contrary, in countries where people are accustomed through
centuries to live at the border of the subsistence level the
marginal rate of saving may even be high.

This idea means first that we have to demonstrate
that the assumption in the Harrod-Domar model—that
the capital coefficient remains constant over time—is of
no use for the explanation of economic progress, because as long as the capital-output ratio remains con-

stant it is only through an increase in the rate of investment that the growth situation may come to an end. The
assumption of the constancy of the capital coefficient
means that it is taken for granted that only through an
increase in capital intensity K/L, labor productivity
Y/L can go up. In order to demonstrate this we have
only to write the capital coefficient in a somewhat different way.[11]

$$\frac{K}{Y} = \frac{K}{L} \cdot \frac{L}{Y}$$

or

$$\frac{K}{Y} = \frac{K/L}{Y/L}$$

or

$$\text{Capital coefficient} = \frac{\text{Capital intensity}}{\text{Labor productivity}}$$

Thus, assuming that the capital-output ratio remains
constant means assuming that only through an increase
in capital intensity can labor productivity increase. But
then only through saving and investment can labor
productivity and thus per capita income go up. Even
Adam Smith, however, knew better. The first sentence
of the first chapter of the first book of the *Wealth of Nations* reads: ". . . the greatest improvement in the
productive power of labour . . . seem to have been the
effects of the division of labour." And he continues: "I
have seen a small pin factory where ten men only were
employed. . . . But though they were *very poor, and
therefore but indifferently accommodated with the necessary machinery* [italics added], they could make
among them upwards of forty-eight thousand pins a day.
But if they had all wrought separately and independ-
ently, and without any of them having been educated to
this peculiar business, they certainly could not each
of them have made twenty, perhaps not one pin a
day. . . ."

Translated into modern economic jargon, this means that even with a low capital intensity ("indifferently accommodated with machinery"), labor productivity can increase, through a better organization of labor.* We will see in Chapter 5 that in the Japanese textile industry during the period 1886-90 to 1911-15 the capital intensity remained constant, whereas labor productivity rose with about 80 per cent. Thus the capital-output ratio went down; in other words, out of one additional unit of capital a greater increase in output was produced.

But then we are allowed to drop the assumption of complete complementarity between the factors of production and open the door for a substitution. By doing so we can no longer state bluntly that (disguised) unemployment in low-income countries implies a lack of the complementary factor of production—capital, but we should also take into consideration the possibility that the unemployment is due to an insufficient organization of the existing agents of production.

Being able to explain economic growth in certain parts of the world with the aid of the Harrod-Domar model means only that the assumption of complete complementarity is a good first approximation to explain what really happened in those areas. The existence of complete complementarity, however, can also be understood in terms of an inefficient organization of labor.

In order to show this, we have to introduce the concepts isoquant and isocosts.[12]

Isoquants are production-indifference curves, showing the different combinations of factors of production (e.g., of labor and capital) which can produce given quantities of a special product. The slope of an isoquant thus expresses the rate at which one factor of production can be substituted for another without changing output (see Fig. 4.3, Q and Q_1). The isoquant to the right of another shows the combinations of two factors which

* Because division of labor—within the plant—is not possible without organization of labor.

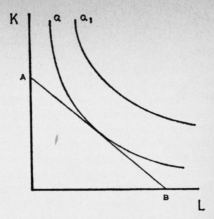

FIG. 4.3   Isoquant and isocost

give a greater quantity of the special product, than the combinations which make up the isoquant to its left.

Given an isocost AB (a line representing the relative prices of the two factors by its slope, and indicating all combinations of the two factors that could be bought for a given sum), and given the production indifference curves, the entrepreneur will find the point where to maximize his profits at a point of tangency between an isoquant and an isocost, because at such points a given isocost comes into contact with the highest isoquant (maximum output at given costs) and a given isoquant comes into contact with the lowest isocost (given output at minimum costs).

Or, the entrepreneur's profit is at a maximum if— given the prices of the two factors of production (e.g., of labor and of capital)—the price ratio between the two factors equals the marginal rate of substitution of the two factors. It is important, however, to note that the number of production processes, where labor and capital can be substituted at will without influencing the quality of the product, is rather limited. Leaving unanswered the question whether the quality of the product will be changed for the better or not, one is able to say that it will change most of the time. In the rather few cases, however, in which substitution of factors of production will not affect the quality of the product, we find in reality not an unlimited scale of variations, but only a small number of technically possible combinations of the production factors.[13] With regard to Fig. 4.3, this implies that in reality we are not concerned with a continuous production indifference *curve,* but with a number of given technical possibilities of combinations of production factors between which we have to make a choice. But given this limited choice, the price ratio of the two factors of production—i.e., the ratio between labor costs and capital costs—determines which technical combination of factors of production at a certain time in a certain country will have to be chosen.

Transportation is one of the production processes in which changes in the combination of factors of production will not be followed by changes in the quality of the final product. Whether commodities are transported by road or by rail will not change the transportation service as such, although the labor-capital combination can be completely different, and the one may be quicker than the other. A very interesting case of substitution possibilities in the field of transportation has been studied by Dr. F. Ritter.[14]

Ritter investigated the various technical combinations, which in Germany by the building of the autobahn were used for transporting 3,000,000 cubic meters of sand over a distance of 600 meters. A working quantity of this size had to be chosen, because with a smaller quantity certain capital-intensive combinations could not be used. Such quantities, however, repeatedly had to be transported by the construction of the autobahn, whereas it should be noted, that because of various work-creating schemes in certain cases methods of a very labor-intensive kind were used as well. Ritter made an analysis of seven technical possibilities which were applied in practice and added two other methods (the scraper type Lorain C 108 and type

Lorain TS 300) which were, it is true, not in use in Germany in the period under consideration (because they did not yet exist!) but for which labor cost and capital cost could be theoretically calculated. The following production processes were investigated:

I   Digging with spades, transport by narrow-gauge dumpers, moved by manpower;

II   Digging with spades, transport via conveyor to the dumpers, moved by manpower;

III   See II; but manpower is replaced by a locomotive;

IV   Clamshells with capacity of 0.35 cu m; transport, see III;

V   Clamshells with capacity of 0.90 cu m; transport, see III;

VI   Clamshells with capacity of 1.35 cu m; transport, see III;

VII   Clamshells with capacity of 1.80 cu m; transport, see III;

VIII   Three scrapers type Lorain C 108; capacity of 8.4 cu m;

IX   Three scrapers type Lorain TS 300; capacity of 13.4 cu m.

For the cost calculation the prices were all deflated to the level of 1950 (so that the *real costs* are under consideration). In Table 4.1, for convenience the costs are computed for the transport of 1,000 cubic meters over a distance of 600 meters, whereby it should be noted that in reality the greater part of the given labor-capital combinations could not be used in transporting of such small quantities.

It is evident that by the then-prevailing costs/capital costs (i.e., wages/interest) ratio, Process VI will give the minimum-cost combination (compare Fig. 4.4).

Processes VIII and IX were definitely superior from a *technical* point of view, but because they were more expensive, they were not rational from an economic point of view. This does not mean that at the same mo-

Table 4.1

CAPITAL-COST—LABOR-COST RELATIONS

(by the Transport of 1,000 cubic meters of Sand Over a Distance of 600 meters (1950 Deutsche Mark)

Production Method	Capital Costs	Labor Costs	Total
I	326	4,440	4,766
II	442	3,895	4,297
III	542	2,485	3,027
IV	1,260	1,088	2,348
V	1,099	896	1,955
VI	1,022	799	1,821
VII	1,330	765	2,095
VIII	1,635	400	2,035
IX	2,005	372	2,377

ment they might not have been economically applied in the United States, where the wage rate was higher and the interest rate lower than in Germany.

When wages are high and the rate of interest low, the tendency to substitute (expensive) labor through (cheap) capital will be strong. Technical improvements that, with relatively low capital cost, make relatively expensive labor superfluous, are therefore rational

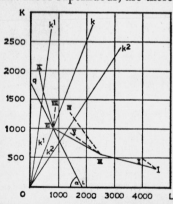

FIG. 4.4 Isoquant for the transport of 1,000 cubic meters of sand over a distance of 600 meters

from an economic point of view. Because in the past hundred years capital has accumulated faster than labor, capitalistic technology has developed in a laborsaving direction. But this does not mean that technical inventions being rational at the existing wage-interest ratio in the United States are also applicable in low-income countries where wages are low and the rate of interest is high.

As far as Processes II, IV, and VII are concerned, they are inefficient under all conditions: even with a change in the wage-interest ratio they will never be rational. However, this is only known *ex post*—i.e., after technology has developed new possibilities, that is to say after Processes III, V, and VIII have come into existence.

In reality we will always find some inefficient process, because some firms still possess certain machines that they want to write off before replacing them by more efficient ones.

We can derive from Fig. 4.4 that the lowest cost combination may shift in two ways that are fundamentally different.[15]

(*a*) Given the price ratio of the factors of production—i.e., given the slope *a* of qL—costs will decrease if technical progress brings about the possibility of a new combination of the factors of production at the left side of qL. We return to this problem in Chapter 6, but let us follow here Ott and distinguish three possibilities:

(1) At the left side of qL, but on k (that is, more product at the same capital intensity);

(2) At the left side of qL and at the left side of k—that is, more product with relatively less labor (k').

(3) At the left side of qL, but at the right side of k—that is, more product with relatively less capital (k^2).

In the rich countries, technical progress has moved in the past century continuously in the direction of k'. However, it is dangerous for the low-income countries to apply the outcomes of this tendency gratuitously. This does not mean, of course, that poor countries should stick to their traditional methods of production (which are, by the way, often rather expensive), but they should try to develop technical progress in a direction that asks for relatively little (expensive) capital and for relatively much (cheap) labor. After all this means nothing else but applying one of the most fundamental principles of economic thinking.

Unfortunately, many of the poor countries have no choice, for the rich, machine-producing countries export *their* machines only—machines that give the most rational combination of the factors of production *in the rich* countries. But such equipment is, by definition, too capital-intensive for the poorer areas. It would be of great help for the poor countries if the highly industrialized would start the design and the production of equipment adopted to the factor price ratio in low-income countries.* The Philips factory in Eindhoven has started a Pilot Plant in Utrecht where production techniques are worked out for developing countries where outputs are much smaller than in the European market. Hence, the division of labor and the specialization of tools cannot be pushed forward as far as in high income countries. It turned out that multi-purpose tools can be profitably applied much more often than highly specialized capital intensive tools when production series are short.

(*b*) The second possibility is a change in the factor price ratio without any change in technology, although this is not very likely in highly industrialized countries because there technology adapts itself continuously at

---

* P. Rosenstein-Rodan once suggested that the Nobel Peace Prize should be given to the man who had done most to change technical progress in the direction of the more labor-intensive processes.

changes in this ratio. However, it follows from Fig. 4.4 that with given technical possibility the slope of qL determines which combination will be the most rational from an economic point of view.

Let us assume that labor costs will only be 10 per cent of the costs indicated in Table 4.1, and let us assume also that they will be twice as high. Table 4.2 demonstrates how total costs and hence the lowest cost combination will change as a result of the shifts.

Table 4.2

Methods of Production	Capital Costs	Labor Costs (1/10 of Those in Table 4.1)	Total Costs	Labor Costs (2 × Costs of Table 4.1)	Total Costs
I	326	444	770	8,880	9,206
II	422	390	812	7,790	8,212
III	542	249	791	4,970	5,512
IV	1,260	109	1,369	2,176	3,436
V	1,099	90	1,189	1,792	2,891
VI	1,022	80	1,102	1,598	2,620
VII	1,330	77	1,407	1,530	2,860
VIII	1,635	40	1,675	800	2,435
IX	2,005	37	2,042	744	2,749

We see, that as labor becomes relatively cheaper, the minimum-cost combination will shift in the direction of the more labor-intensive techniques. This is nothing less than saying that, when capital gets relatively more expensive, technically less efficient processes become economically more rational. On the other hand, we see that as labor gets relatively more expensive, the minimum-cost combination shifts in the direction of the more capital-intensive processes. Thus when capital gets relatively cheaper technically, more efficient processes become economically more rational.

Table 4.2 shows that if only wages would fall low enough, Process I would become economically the most rational production method, and if only wages would rise high enough (or if the rate of interest would fall relatively enough) Process VIII (and at a further shift in the ratio most certainly also Process IX) would become economically the most rational.

The great scarcity of labor in relation to land in the United States in the last century has certainly spurred technical progress to a large degree. In Western Europe industry was able to absorb large quantities of cheap agrarian labor, but industry in the United States had to compete with the alternative available to immigrants— i.e., settling on the land as a farmer. American industry therefore was obliged to pay higher wages than European industry, and the continuous introduction of more laborsaving machinery enabled American entrepreneurs to pay wages that made settlement on (free) land no more attractive. In Europe, where labor was abundant as compared with the States, technological progress lagged behind, but this was not so much due to the greater abilities of American entrepreneurs as to the fundamental differences in factor endowment.[16]

We may observe the same tendency in the private households. Because personnel became very expensive in the United States, laborsaving machinery made its appearance in the households as well (vacuum cleaners, dishwashers, etc.). In Europe where wages of personnel were rather low, demand for this equipment remained low, until after the war when wages of personnel rose considerably. But it would be of course an economic stupidity to introduce these laborsaving devices in countries where unskilled labor is abundant and cheap.

We may therefore conclude that as long as labor is abundant, where disguised unemployment is great, labor-intensive production processes (i.e., processes with a low capital coefficient) have to be sponsored as much as possible. This requires great organizational capacities, but it certainly serves to sponsor economic development. It seems that in China this policy has been widely adopted. In North-Kiangso, for example, 2.5 billion cubic feet of land were transported in 80 days for the construction of irrigation works by 1.3 million laborers who were seasonally unemployed.[17]

CHANGING THE COMPOSITION OF INVESTMENT

Thus far we dealt with the *overall* (the macroeconomic) capital coefficient only. Our argument has been that if we are able to increase labor productivity, through a better organization of labor—i.e., without a proportional increase in capital intensity, the capital output ratio will fall. It goes without saying that with a given rate of savings and a given rate of increase in population, this might mean the end of the growth situation and the beginning of economic development. However, under certain conditions the government has another mighty weapon for lowering the capital coefficient. The rich people in the poor countries (mentioned above) most of the time invest at home practically only in residential construction. We think that one of the reasons why they do so is that one does not need any managerial capacity to let a block of flats. Furthermore, in many poor countries ownership of land is important for somebody's social status, and so is the ownership of houses.

Because in many low-income countries 50 per cent and more of net investment is invested in residential construction, and because the capital coefficient of investments of this type is about 8, it is clear that a change in the composition of investment may have a considerable effect on the average capital-output ratio.

Assume that the average capital-output ratio $= k = 3.3$, that of residential construction $= k_1 = 8.0$, and that of the balance $= k_2 = 2.1$. If 50 per cent (out of an investment of 100) is invested in construction, we find the following equation:

$$k = \frac{k}{y} = \frac{k_1 + k_2}{y_1 + y_2} = \frac{k_1}{y_1 + y_2} + \frac{k_2}{y_1 + y_2}$$

$$= \frac{y_1}{y_1 + y_2} \cdot \frac{k_1}{y_1} + \frac{y_2}{y_1 + y_2} \cdot \frac{k_2}{y_2}$$

$$= \frac{y_1}{y_1 + y_2} \cdot k_1 + \frac{y_2}{y_1 + y_2} \cdot k_2$$

$$k = \frac{50 + 50}{6.25 + 23.75} = \frac{100}{30} = 3.3$$

If, however, only 20 per cent is invested in construction and 80 per cent at a capital-output ratio of 2.1, the equation becomes:

$$k = \frac{20 + 80}{2.5 + 38.0} = \frac{100}{40.5} = 2.5$$

Through such a policy the capital-output ratio would thus drop from 3.3 to 2.5. Instead of the numerical example of Mahalanobis:

$$0.25 = \frac{5}{3.3} - 1.25$$

we would get

$$0.75 = \frac{5}{2.5} - 1.25$$

That is, instead of an annual increase in per capita income of 0.25 per cent we would find 0.75 per cent. Of course this depends on the willingness of the rich to invest in directions other than construction, and we have already pointed out that we are not too optimistic in this respect.

But we have explained in any case why in rapidly expanding economies we normally find a low rate of residential construction and a great housing shortage.

INCREASING THE CAPITAL-OUTPUT RATIO

Against our opinion that a country that tries to break through the low-per-capita-income growth situation should keep its capital-output ratio as low as possible, R. Bićanić assumes that the economic development phase is coupled with a rapid increase in the capital-output ratio. "It can therefore be described more real-

Table 4.3

INCOME PER CAPITA (IN DOLLARS) AND CAPITAL
COEFFICIENTS FOR VARIOUS COUNTRIES

	Japan		Sweden		Denmark		Australia		Canada	
Year	Y/P	$\Delta K/\Delta Y$	Y/P	$\Delta K/\Delta Y$	Y/P	$\Delta K/\Delta Y$	Y/P	$\Delta K/\Delta Y$	Y/P	$\Delta K/\Delta Y$
1860							450	1.4	280	0.6
1880	45	1.0	170	2.1	240	1.1	480	1.6	390	0.6
1900	65	1.6	260	2.1	340	1.8	500	3.3	550	1.0
1913	90	2.0	420	2.2	430	2.2	590	—	700	—
1929	140	2.1	560	—	610	2.7	660	3.6	850	1.7
1953	180	3.7	940	3.9	740	4.9	960	5.7	1300	3.3

istically as a painful process of creeping over the threshold of economic growth, rather than an elegant 'takeoff,' which does not adequately convey the difficulty and intensity of the problems of this stage." [18]

In order to realize then a 0.75 annual percentage increase in per capita income we would need a rate of investment of 12, because

$$0.75 = \frac{12}{6} - 1.25$$

A growth rate of national income of 5 per cent, observed in various developing countries, would then require a rate of investment of 30.

M. H. Khan, in an unpublished thesis (Institute of Social Studies), compared my figures on per capita income (Y/P, as published in Chapter 2) with Kuznets's data on incremental capital-output ratios ($\Delta K/\Delta Y$),[19] with the results as shown in Table 4.3, (p. 93 above). Because all countries mentioned in Table 4.3 went through a process of economic development during the period 1870-1913, it is clear that, so far as *they* are concerned, the capital-output ratio was very *low* during this process. Bićanić assumes further that once the period of economic development is over, the capital coefficient will fall. Our data are also here in complete contradiction with his assumption. Only in the United States a falling capital-output ratio has been observed over the last decades.

CONCLUSION

Our approach to the problem of economic growth differs fundamentally from that of the classical economists. We have taken the increase in population as an independent variable, and asked how much investment is needed with a given capital intensity in order to guarantee constant per capita income. We have taken for granted that additional labor can always be employed, provided enough organizational talent and/or additional investment are available. We found that, with a constant capital-output ratio, capital has to increase in the same proportion as population in order to keep per capita income constant. Malthus, however, asked what would happen with per capita income when population increased and capital (i.e., land) and technology remained constant.[20]

Due to the law of diminishing returns, per capita income had to fall in the long run. (We asked: How many complementary means of production are needed in order to avoid such a fall?).

Malthus thus assumed that per capita income ($Y/P = y$) was a monotonic-decreasing function of P:[21]

$$y = gP$$

He assumed further that population will increase as long as y is greater than the subsistence level (y'), whereas population will decrease in the case that $y < y'$ (our constant per capita income in the low-income countries is about equal to y'). If the numerical value of the net reproduction rate r is greater or smaller than 1, population will increase or decrease. At $r = 1$ population will remain constant. According to Malthus, r is a function of ($y - y_1$), the greater the difference the greater r will be. At $y = y_1$, $r = 1$, at $y > y'$, $r > 1$ and at $y < y'$, $r < 1$. At $y = y'$, i.e., at $r = 1$, the population is in equilibrium—that is, it remains constant. This is the so-called Malthusian low-per-capita-income equilibrium.

We have given a somewhat different interpretation of this equilibrium because today it is known that in many countries even at $y = y'$ population continued to increase, which can be explained only if we assume that every additional laborer acquired exactly the same amount of capital as his predecessors.

At a very low income level a small increase in (agrarian) production and therefore in consumption leads almost immediately to an increase in population—not so much as a result of the increase in the birthrate as by a fall in the deathrate (and particularly in infant mortal-

ity). In England, for example, the population increased
from 11 to 16.5 million during the period 1801-31, the
birthrate dropped, however, but the death rate dropped
more.[22]

Especially in agrarian communities small increases in
production therefore do not lead to a continuous increase in per capita income. In Java, for example, rice
production increased by 140 per cent during the period
1880-1940, but as population increased at exactly the
same rate, per capita rice consumption remained constant.

Malthus assumed that in agrarian societies with an
increase in population the land-man ratio will fall. This
is certainly not an unrealistic assumption: in India, for
example, the land-man ratio dropped by 23 per cent
during the period 1891-1951. Because it is not so much
the difference in farm income per acre but the average
size of the farm that causes the huge regional differences
in farm income, the deterioration of the land-man ratio
has a very unfavorable impact on the per capita agrarian income.

Although the data in Table 4.4 are rather old (they
are expressed in 1930 prices) they may be considered
nevertheless as an illustration of a situation that still
exists today.[23]

Table 4.4
FARM INCOMES (CA. 1930)

Country	Income per Acre, Dollars	Average Size of Farm in Acre	Average Farm Income, Dollars
United States	$ 25	303	$1,230
Denmark	135	35	790
North China	151	4	100
Java	136	4	100

In very densely populated agrarian areas, the yield
per acre is not affected by the size of the farm. According to Colin Clark[24] it did not make any difference in the

yield per acre in China if the size of the farm was 0.53 or 1.25 acre. In other words, the marginal productivity of labor on land was zero on the very small farms.

Because no employment possibilities are available in the secondary sector in many of the low-income countries, we find a huge outflux of agrarian population to the tertiary sector. The great amount of very small shops, characteristic for all low-income countries, is nothing but an indication of the availability of disguised unemployment. The percentage distribution of the labor force over the primary, secondary, and tertiary sector in Egypt clearly demonstrates this (Table 4.5). It is therefore not so much the percentage decline

Table 4.5

PERCENTAGE DISTRIBUTION OF THE LABOR FORCE
IN EGYPT, 1907-60

	Agriculture	*Industry*	*Services*
1907	71	11	18
1937	71	10	19
1947	64	12	24
1960	58	12	32

in employment in agriculture, but the increase in percentage employment in industry that counts.

One of the main topics of economic analysis is the equilibrium situation, and economists have always been very fond of *built-in stabilizers*. The gold standard is an excellent example.

Keynes, however, drew our attention to undesirable equilibrium situations—e.g., the stable underemployment equilibrium; also, the Malthusian low-per-capita-income equilibrium may be considered as very undesirable. Destabilizers thus become very important. Harvey Leibenstein[25] has indicated under what special conditions the Malthusian equilibrium does not need to be stable. Those conditions are illustrated in Fig. 4.5. In the left-hand and right-hand parts of the graph, per capita income is plotted on the ordinate, and y' is the

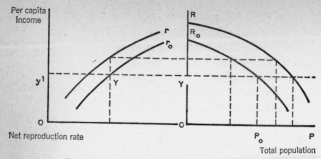

FIG. 4.5 Conditions for unstable Malthusian distribution

subsistence minimum. The net reproduction rate is plotted on the abscissae of the left, and on the right, total
population. The r_0 function in the left-hand part indicates the relation between net reproduction and per capita income. At y' the net reproduction is equal to 1, no
further increase in population (OP_0 in the right-hand
part) takes place, the Malthusian equilibrium is reached.
The R_0 function in the right-hand part indicates how,
with a given amount of natural resources, per capita income falls* when population increases.† This continues
until the point is reached where the land-man ratio
guarantees the subsistence minimum and nothing more
(at a population of OP_0). Thus when population has increased to OP_0, the agrarian population lives at a level
y', and $r = 1$—i.e., the population remains constant.

According to Malthus, this is the only possibility. For
if the R function shifts to the right, per capita income
will increase temporarily and, in the long run, population will increase until it again becomes equal to y'. But
—and this possibility was overlooked by Malthus—if
before y' is reached, the R function again shifts to the
right, per capita income can continue to increase. In
other words, we can escape from the Malthusian equi-

---

* One might also say the land-man ratio will fall.
† As far as we know, only in Ireland population has decreased continuously, but not as a result of the decline in the
birthrate but through emigration.

librium if the increase in available resources surpasses the increase in population.

According to Leibenstein, a relatively small increase in resources will normally lead to an equivalent increase in population. With a rather great increase in capital* only, the percentage increase in income could also and in the long run surpass the increase in population.

However, most of the poor countries are faced in the postwar period with a rather serious complication. Because it is relatively cheap to control contagious diseases, many of the low-income countries have shown a rather heavy fall in the deathrate, whereas the birthrate has remained constant, hence a rapid increase in population took place.

In Ceylon for instance the increase in population was 1.7 per cent per annum during the period 1931-46, against 2.8 per cent from 1946-51; in British Guiana the population increase doubled after the war. Under those conditions a rather important increase in national income does not need to lead to an increase in per capita income. On the contrary, those countries, like the Red Queen, have to run fast in order to stay in the same place. We may mention here countries like Ceylon, Malaya, Nigeria, and Guatemala, where, according to Reports of the International Bank for Reconstruction and Development rather important increases in national income will not result in increases in per capita income, due to the rapid increase in population.

For Egypt we found, when applying the formula

$$\dot{y} = \frac{s}{x} - p$$

for the period 1913-53

$$- 0.6 = \frac{4.9}{3.5} - 2.0$$

---

* It follows from what we said before that here certainly should be added: and organizational talent.

After 1953 the increase in population was still greater, and at an annual increase of 3 per cent, net investment has to be even greater than 10 per cent in order to keep per capita income constant. Transferring a growth situation into one of economic progress becomes very difficult indeed under such unfavorable conditions.

NOTES

1. We may do this as a first approximation, but a certain relationship between the age composition of a society and its per capita income exists. Compare R. Olivier, *Planification en Afrique, II*, 1963, p. 28: Ministère de la Coopération, Centre de Documentation:

Country		Percentage Age Distribution			Number of Persons Supported by One Adult
		0-20	20-65	65 and Over	
United Kingdom	1955	29.2	59.5	11.3	1.68
Norway	1953	30.9	58.6	10.5	1.70
France	1956	31.1	57.3	11.6	1.75
Denmark	1954	33.5	56.9	9.6	1.76
United States	1954	35.8	55.7	8.5	1.79
New Zealand	1954	37.7	53.2	9.6	1.88
India	1957	47.5	48.9	3.6	2.05
Turkey	1955	49.7	47.0	3.3	2.13
Peru	1955	54.7	42.5	3.0	2.36

2. Compare R. F. Harrod, *Towards a Dynamic Economics* (1948), and E. D. Domar, "Expansion and Employment," *American Economic Review,* March 1947.

3. Compare J. H. Power, "Capital Intensity and Economic Growth," *American Economic Review,* May 1955, p. 198.

4. Compare W. Navarette and I. M. Navarette, "Underemployment in Underdeveloped Economies," in *International Economic Papers* (1953).

5. P. C. Mahalanobis, "National Income, Investment and National Development," Lecture at the National Institute of Sciences of India, October 1952.

6. Compare W. W. Rostow, *The Stages of Economic Growth* (1960), p. 39 ("progress" in our terminology).

7. Compare E. E. Hagen, *On the Theory of Social Change* (1962), Chap. 3, "Inadequacy of Economic Theories of Growth."

8. W. A. Lewis, *The Theory of Economic Growth* (1955), p. 236.

9. E. E. Hagen, *op. cit.*, p. 39.

10. E. E. Hagen, *op. cit.*, pp. 305, 351.

11. K. K. Kurihara, *The Keynesian Theory of Economic Development* (1959), p. 94.

12. Every economic textbook deals with the problem of the optimal combination of the factors of production; see T. Scitovsky, *Welfare and Competition* (1955).

13. The division of Industrial Development of the United Nations has done very interesting research in this direction. Some of the results are published regularly in the United Nation's bulletin, *Industrialization and Productivity*.

14. F. Ritter, "Die technische Auswirkung progressiver Investierung an einem Element der Bauwirtschaft," unpublished thesis, Mainz University, 1952.

15. Compare A. F. Ott, *Production Functions, Technical Progress, and Economic Growth*, International Papers, 1962.

16. Compare J. H. Habbakuk, "Population Growth and Economic Development," in *Lectures on Economic Development* (Istanbul, 1958), p. 33, and E. Rothbarth, "Causes of Superior Efficiency of U.S.A. Industry as Compared with British Industry," *Economic Journal*, 1946, pp. 383-390. It goes without saying that factor endowment is not the same all over the United States. According to G. J. Stigler (*Theory of Price*, 1947, p. 111) the same amount of corn per acre was produced in Kansas and Texas with 2.2 man-hours and much machinery against 22.8 man-hours and little machinery in Georgia. Here technology was adopted at the factor price ratio, but—more important—the example demonstrated that it is possible to produce under completely different technology and nevertheless compete in the same market.

17. Compare "Capital Intensity in Heavy Engineering Construction," in United Nations' bulletin *Industrialization and Productivity*, April 1958, p. 37; according to W. Malenbaum, in "India and China: Contrasts in Development Per-

formance," *American Economic Review,* June 1959, the capital output ratio in China has been 2.2, against 4.0 in India.

18. R. Bićanić, "The Threshold of Economic Growth," *Kyklos,* 1962, No. 1, p. 19.

19. S. S. Kuznets, "Quantitative Aspects of the Economic Growth of Nations: VI. Long-Term Trends in Capital Formation Proportions," in *Economic Development and Cultural Change,* July 1961, Tables 3 and 7, pp. 10-11, 22-24.

20. A rather unrealistic assumption in the Malthusian epoch if one realizes that in the eighteenth century agrarian productivity rose considerably in England. From a few estimates communicated by Colin Clark on the World Population Congress in Tokyo in 1957 we constructed the following table:

CORN YIELD IN ENGLAND

Year	Bushels per Acre
1350	5.5
1450	6.5
1550	7.5
1650	8.5
1750	12.5
1800	20.0
1950	40.0

21. We follow here K. E. Boulding, "The Malthusian Model as a General System," in *Social and Economic Studies* (Jamaica, 1955), p. 191; compare W. J. Baumol, *Economic Dynamics* (1959), p. 19.

22. Compare G. Talbot Griffith, *Population Problems in the Age of Malthus* (1926).

23. Compare E. de Vries, "Beschouwingen over de inlandse landbouw en het loonpeil op Java en Madoera," in *Koloniale Studiën,* June 1932, p. 269.

24. Communication on the World Population Conference, Tokyo, 1957.

25. Harvey Leibenstein, *Theory of Economic-Demographic Development* (1954).

Chapter 5

ECONOMIC DEVELOPMENT

In his *Aspects of the Novel*,[1] E. M. Forster makes a distinction between the *story* and the *plot* of a novel. A story is a narrative of events arranged in their time sequence;[2] a plot is also a narrative of events but the emphasis falls on causality.[3] The novel has two fundamentally different aspects: so far as the story is concerned we ask, "What happened next," and as to the plot we ask, "Why did it happen?" We use this distinction as an introduction because we think that it is not too difficult to tell the story of the economic development of a certain country, but it is often difficult to find the plot. For most economists the story of economic development is a rather simple one. In the beginning we hear that today a considerable part of mankind is still living under conditions of economic growth—i.e., in economic systems with constant per capita incomes. In the preceding chapter we saw that economic growth can be characterized as a situation in which the percentage increase in population p equals the ratio between the average rate of savings s and the capital coefficient k:

$$p = \frac{s}{k}$$

A percentage increase in per capita income $\dot{y}$ can be expressed by the formula

$$\dot{y} = \frac{s}{k} - p$$

Assuming that the capital coefficient is the same all over the world and equal to 3.5 makes it possible to condense the whole story in two formulas—one for the

rich part of the world, the other for the poor. If we consider the period 1913-53 we find for the rich countries:

$$2.1 = \frac{11.5}{3.5} - 1.2$$

and for the poor,

$$0 = \frac{4.9}{3.5} - 1.4$$

Thus in order to transform a situation of economic
growth into a progressing one, the rate of saving and
investment has to increase from about 5 per cent to 10
per cent or more of the national income (W. W. Rostow). But once the story is told we have to agree with
Meier and Baldwin that economic development is much
too serious a topic to be left to economists.[4] For the increase in investment is only one aspect of a huge process
of overall social change that took place in certain countries. For us the most fascinating question seems to be,
why did it happen in certain areas and not in others? We
will try in this chapter to detect the plot in the story of
economic development of two countries which are spectacular examples of successful development—England
in the second half of the eighteenth century and Japan
in the second half of the nineteenth century.

Before going on, however, a few words must be
added to Rostow's story. We have seen that an increase in income can also come about through a decrease in the numerical value of the capital coefficient.
Because this is possible as a result of better organization of production, management (entrepreneurship)
can substitute for capital. If the energies and ingenuity
of the people are mobilized, more can be produced with
the given resources.[5] The same is of course true for the
individual enterprise and we consider this *Horndal-
effect*[6] of paramount importance for the theory of economic development, because it demonstrates that the
individual plant as well as a country does not need to
have a high average rate of saving and investment in

order to *start* economic development. The combination of managerial ability and a high *marginal* propensity to save is, even in a very low-income country, a sufficient condition to start economic progress.

The foregoing is of great significance for our theory of economic progress because in the eighteenth century Western countries were certainly not richer than the rest of the world. And because the poor countries have shown but very little progress in the past centuries, we are entitled to say that they were not much richer at the time than the poor countries are today. With the aid of the data collected by Phyllis Dean we made an estimate of the per capita income in the United Kingdom in the beginning of the eighteenth century (Table 5.1). At

---

Table 5.1

PER CAPITA INCOME IN THE UNITED KINGDOM, 1700-1960[7]

Year	Per Capita Income in 1952-54 Dollars	Year	Per Capita Income in 1952-54 Dollars
1960	$910	1875-84	$310
1957	860	1870	260
1952-54	780	1860	260
1946-52	720	1850	240
1935-44	680	1839	180
1925-34	550	1820	150
1915-24	480	1812	110
1905-14	480	1800	110
1895-1904	450	1744	70
1885-94	390	1695	60

---

the end of the seventeenth century Gregory King made an estimate of the national income not only for the United Kingdom, but also for France and Holland. Applying his findings to the per capita income of $60 for the United Kingdom gives us for Holland $60 as well, against $50 in France.[8]

Although these estimates are very rough indeed, we are nevertheless entitled to say that at the eve of the industrial revolution Western Europe had a very low income—i.e., it was very poor to begin with.[9] But as soon as we assume that the great masses in the Western European countries lived for centuries near the physical existence minimum,* the problem of Western economic development not only becomes much more interesting but also gains in actuality.

Nowadays it has become a platitude to state that poor countries are too poor to accumulate enough capital and therefore remain poor. But if Western countries, starting poor, were able in the past to increase their rates of investment considerably, it is worthwhile to find out how they did it. Perhaps poor countries today can learn something from this.

We first of all have to describe what happened in England and Japan during the process of economic development and then try to discover the "plot."

We are aware that this approach involves a danger. In trying to find the plot we are more or less in the position of the reader of a detective story, who first looks at the last page to find out "who committed the crime," and thereafter is able to find page after page of indications leading to the solution. Because we know that the process of economic development both in England and Japan was successful, we run the risk of interpreting their development as inevitable: conditions were extremely favorable, people were exceptionally capable, etc.

But because both England and Japan for centuries had a practically constant, low per capita income we have to answer the question, why did capable men appear rather suddenly, and why did they *see* favorable possibilities? For possibilities never exist, they are created by man.[10]

Creation of new possibilities means change, and as a point of departure in the analysis of economic development we wish to introduce the thesis that traditional man does not like change, and in fact resists change. In a traditional society the desire among the younger

* Classical economists took this for granted.

generation to be more or less different from the older generation on the whole is very weak.[11]

We do not need to cite as examples the worshipping of ancestors nor the role that tradition plays in Islam, one simply has to look at a few eighteenth-century Western European family portraits to observe that "young people" * were dressed and behaved in complete conformity with the older ones. This was a social attitude: things were good *because* they had been done already for a long time.

Then it becomes clear why in the past most societies —leaders as well as led—have not been capable of adapting themselves to fundamentally new conditions.[12] The history of man is a graveyard of great cultures that came to catastrophic ends because of their incapacity for planned, rational, voluntary reaction to challenge.[13] We know of cultures that disappeared because climatological conditions changed, because trade routes changed, etc. To quote Fromm again: "Even when circumstances that were in complete and flagrant contradiction to their whole structure arose, such societies went on blindly trying to continue their modes of living until they could not manage any further." [14]

Some rulers have been aware of this fact and have tried to make their people change-minded. Peter the Great who personally cut the beards of his bojars and Kemal Ataturk who banished the fez are famous examples. For modern man in the West, who has succeeded in living more or less harmoniously in a changing environment, it is difficult to understand that a change in hairdress or in a hat could ever be considered as a revolutionary act. But this lack of comprehension indicates exactly the cultural difference between a traditional society where children behave like their parents and the modern Western society where parents do their utmost to behave like their children.†

* The "child" has been invented only recently.

† After having spent one day on a camping site the reader will agree that this thesis is justified.

In Western countries this process took at least 150 years. However, one will never understand economic development if one continues to think in quantitative terms of 5 or 10 per cent investment only, without understanding the enormous resistance nonconformists —the independent thinkers who wanted to analyze their problems themselves[15]—had to overcome before a traditional society could be changed into a dynamic one.*

The challenge that may lead to change is sometimes caused by endogenous, sometimes by exogenous factors. We shall see that the former was the case in the United Kingdom, the latter in Japan. In both countries a successful response has been given, but it would be wrong to assume that this was due to abundant factor endowment. Only *ex post* one can speak of objective good conditions; *ex ante* it is merely the subjective judgment of man that counts. No theory of economic development is possible unless we view man as the creator of his own environment.[16]

THE CASE OF ENGLAND

The wood shortage that already had become manifest in the United Kingdom during the reign of Queen Elizabeth was the challenge which had to be answered. From 1540 to 1640 the price of wood increased three times as much as the general price level.[17] Wood was needed mainly for construction, for shipbuilding, for fuel and industrial purposes. Shipbuilding was assigned top priority, and by decree all persons were forbidden to cut wood for other purposes within fourteen miles of the coast.[18] This shortage of wood stimulated the tendency to substitute coal for wood in industrial production, and this practice finally led (although it was com-

---

* In a dynamic society the absence of change is considered stagnation: if per capita income does not increase in the modern progressing economy, we speak of a recession.

pletely unforeseen at the time) to the great Industrial Revolution.*

In some industries the substitution, technically speaking, was rather simple—e.g., in brickyards, in breweries, and with the evaporation of salt water.[19] After the introduction of coal in the glass industry the *Proclamation Touching Glasses* (1615) forbade the use of coal in this industry.[20] This prohibition had far-reaching consequences, because the new ovens started to produce window glass, which resulted in a tendency towards mass production in British glassmaking.†

Introduction of coal in so many industries seems to have somewhat diminished the demand for wood, which caused a decline in the tendency to substitute coal for wood in iron production. Another important factor was that charcoal, used in iron production, did not require transportation over long distances (as was the case with fuel for domestic purposes and timber), and therefore increased less in price than did other kinds of fuel.[21] Although it is possible that coal was applied already successfully in the beginning of the seventeenth century in iron production, the technique was lost.[22] Moreover, Darby's experiment of using coke for the melting of iron did not find widespread application in the metallurgical industry.[23]

But step by step the situation in iron production deteriorated, and in the first half of the eighteenth century a definite decline set in (Fig. 5.1). Iron producers were forced to locate their production in the woods, and because more and more woods were cut down the dis-

---

* The name is a misnomer, because it was much more an evolution than a revolution, and at least as much social as industrial.

† In France, where the challenge seems to have been much less pronounced, it was not before 1763 that the famous glass factory of St. Gobain started some experiments with coal, but without success. Even in 1819 the firm bought huge forests to guarantee the supply of fuel. Thus the availability of the traditional factors of production impeded technological progress.

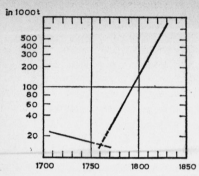

in 1000 t

FIG. 5.1   Iron production in England, Scotland, and Wales
(thousands of tons)

tance between the iron mines and the furnaces, and
hence the cost of transportation, increased continually.
In this period the whole English iron industry was jeopardized. It almost suffered the same fate as did the Russian iron industry in the eighteenth century where unbridled exploitation of the forests of the Ural brought
about the end of iron production.

In England, however, in contrast with Russia, the deposits of iron and coal were near at hand and thus everything depended on the technology of producing iron
with coke. About 1780 Henry Cort solved this problem
with his puddling furnace, and from this moment onwards iron production increased enormously.[24] But this
was nearly 200 years after English producers were confronted for the first time with the problem of the substitution of charcoal.

But iron producers not only were dependent on wood,
they also needed the rivers in South England for power.
Thus it was the combination of (*a*) the substitution of
coal for charcoal and (*b*) the substitution of the steam
engine for water power which made iron producers independent of the woods and rivers. Only after these
problems were solved could the iron industry shift to the
Midlands, to Scotland, Northeast England and South

Wales. In those areas both iron ore and coal were available.[25]

Now one may argue that, after all, it was the favorable factor endowment that made Britain prosperous. But this is reasoning *ex post*. The only thing that really counts is what man makes of his environment. Not the fact that iron ore and coal were *available* but the fact that man was able to *combine* them for the production of iron was important.

Thus far, however, the story is too simple. It is true that the location of iron ore and coal could sponsor the production of iron. They had only to be brought together.

But according to a well-known author writing in the middle of the eighteenth century, the English roads at that time were in the condition in which "God left them after the flood." [26] Daniel Defoe informs us that the transporting of timber from Lewes to Chatham by road took two or three *years*. He saw a cart drawn by twenty-two oxen which transported a tree trunk a few miles, after which the owner had to find another team.[27]

The solution of this transportation problem was, therefore, a precondition for economic development. Coal and iron ore could not be brought together, economically speaking, without a considerable decrease in transport costs. The way in which the British solved this transport problem was of great importance not only for the economic development of the country but also for the future British individualistic approach towards economic matters. Had they not been able to solve this problem without governmental interference, perhaps they would never have had the repugnance against government assistance that is so symptomatic of British classical economy.*

In modern discussions on infrastructural investment

---

* We have to add here, however, that British governments in those days were so impotent that it is difficult to imagine how they could have helped.

in general, and on investment in transport facilities in particular, it is argued over and over again that the direct profits on such investments, supposing they are made, are much lower than the indirect benefits which society as a whole enjoys from those investments. It goes without saying that, as long as direct profits are lower than those made on other investments, no private investor will execute such infrastructural investment, even if indirect benefits might be considerable. The result, then, is that society is deprived of the indirect profits as well. Hence private industry will be devoid of the indirect benefits as long as government does not undertake those projects. Today, all experts on economic development and economic planning advocate the execution of infrastructural investments through, or with the aid of, government. However, in Britain in the eighteenth century it was private enterprise that carried out these projects. They not only made reasonable direct profits on their investments but they received the indirect benefits as well, because they made the infrastructural investments on behalf of their own plans. Thus through those infrastructural investments they created the *external economies* for their own industries. But this again means that they had to create their own environment, that they had to plan ahead and over a long time span.

The first entrepreneur to be mentioned in this connection is the Duke of Bridgewater, who together with James Brindley—a man of genius, who like many other inventors in the eighteenth century, was practically illiterate—constructed in 1760 the first canal in England, from his coal mines in Worsley to Manchester. We consider the Duke as one of the great personalities in British economic history of those days, and if anyone needs a case to prove that "private profit means public benefit" he needs only to mention Bridgewater: after the completion of his canal the price of coal in Manchester was lowered by 50 per cent and the production of his coal-mines increased considerably.

At about the same time Josiah Wedgwood innovated

the pottery industry, but because roads were hopelessly bad, he was practically unable to transport his products (on horseback). Wedgwood became, together with Bridgewater and a few other industrialists from the area, the promoter of the Mersey-Trent canal, later on expanded to the Grand Trunk, which was completed in 1777. According to Wedgwood's communication, about 7,000 people were employed in the Potteries around 1760. In 1785 after the completion of the canals, about 20,000 were employed.[28] Although Marshall chose as the motto for his *Principles of Economics: natura non facit soltum,* one gets the impression that *man* is able to do it, and that this is the secret of economic development.[29] Not by small steps, but by great jumps, by big pushes[30] man had to break through the stationary state of the economy.

The impact on costs of transportation was enormous (compare Table 5.2). Adam Smith already had fully realized this: "Good roads, canals and navigable rivers, by diminishing the expense of carriage, put the remote parts of the country more nearly upon a level with those in the neighborhood of the town. They are upon that account the *greatest of all improvements* [italics

Table 5.2

TRANSPORTATION COSTS PER TON BY LAND AND WATER IN ENGLAND ABOUT 1790 IN POUNDS[31]

Route	By Land	By Water	By Water as a Percentage of by Land
Liverpool-Wolverhampton	£5.0	£1.5	25.0
Birmingham-Gainsborough	3.18	1.0	25.6
Manchester-Potteries	2.15	0.15	27.2
Birmingham-Liverpool	5.0	1.10	30.0
Liverpool-Stourport	5.0	1.10	30.0
Manchester-Stourport	4.13	1.10	32.2
Manchester-Birmingham	4.0	1.10	37.5
Chester-Wolverhampton	3.10	1.15	50.0
Chester-Birmingham	3.10	2.0	57.1

added] . . . they break down monopolies . . . they open new markets. . . ." [32]

The quantitative importance of the decrease in costs of transportation can be demonstrated with data about the development of the breweries in England, because in a brewery large-scale production was possible long before the introduction of the steam engine.[33] Originally the brewer could be compared with a baker: his market had a range of action of three to five miles. With the development of transport in the second half of the eighteenth century we see a rapid decline in local breweries and a quick increase in the big firms[34] (Table 5.3).

Table 5.3

NUMBER OF BREWERIES IN ENGLAND IN THE EIGHTEENTH CENTURY

	Local Breweries	Big Breweries
1700	39,469	746
1750	48,421	996
1799	23,690	1,382

The enlarged market in the literal and in the figurative sense of the word widened the economic horizon of the entrepreneurs. Markets are never "too small" in any objective way; they are too small because certain people at a certain moment believe them to be so.[35] Although infrastructural improvements in the second half of the eighteenth century definitely enlarged the market in an objective way, this does not mean that entrepreneurial activity had to react automatically.[36] But at that time their economic horizon widened indeed, and once this process had set in it became perpetual.

Thus we have seen that in the eighteenth century fundamental technological changes took place. Those technological changes for the economist are somewhat difficult to handle. Economics deals with the optimal al-

location of scarce resources, but, according to Ortega
y Gasset:[37] "technique is the opposite of the adaptation
of the subject to the means, it is the adaptation of the
means to the subject." In economics the environment
is taken as a *datum* but economic development means
changing data, both in the technical as well as in the
psychological field. We think that the wood shortage in
Britain created chain reactions in both spheres of activities. People became convinced that they could respond to the challenge: they wanted to achieve and
they did. They consciously made the infrastructural investments, which are a precondition for wide markets,
and they subsequently took advantage of the enlarged
possibilities. In other words, they created the favorable
conditions which were not there to begin with.

Once the data are changed the economist again feels
on safe grounds. He can now even add a few things.

Infrastructural investments, like those in blast furnaces, rolling mills, mines, etc., require a wide entrepreneurial horizon because the velocity of circulation of
capital in these projects is much slower than that of capital invested in trade.[38] But here the economist is again at
a loss, because the profit motive can never explain to
him why those new dynamic entrepreneurs did not simply go into trade where profits perhaps were even higher
than in industry. We think that McClelland has given
the answer to this question:[39] "Many of the industrial innovators did not seem to be motivated primarily by the
desire for money as such; if they had been, many of
them ought to have quit working sooner; often they had
made all the money they could possibly use. . . . Still
others, the Quakers and dissenters in England, for example, must have had a very peculiar kind of interest in
money indeed, since they were prevented by religious
scruples from spending it in any of the many delightful
ways employed by the continental nobility at the time.
. . . But Western capitalists were not interested in
money and profit for its own sake. To them it was the

measure of success. It gave them the concrete knowledge of the outcome of their efforts that their motivation
demanded."

But this also explains why they plowed back considerable portions of their profits into their enterprises.
They were people with imagination who saw the possibility of breaking through the stationary state by changing the environment. They understood that, in order to
continue, the marginal rate of saving had to be high, and
they therefore tried to keep the level of consumption
more or less constant. This was the attitude of British
Puritans in the eighteenth century, of the Japanese samurai in the nineteenth and of the Soviet ruling class in
the twentieth century. They all tried to increase labor
productivity, they sponsored technological change and
they kept the level of consumption low in order to increase capital formation.

As soon as we deal with economic development in
other countries than England, technical problems become less important. The others were able to apply the
final results of English experiments,* whereas the British started in the nineteenth century also to introduce
their inventions on the European continent and to give
technical assistance to many countries. Countries like
Japan and the Soviet Union could start with the introduction of techniques developed by others. We mention this
not to deprecate the achievements in these countries, but
to point up the fact that they succeeded where many
others failed—demonstrating first of all that they were
able to adapt technology to their own conditions, and
secondly that their innovators had the energy and the
political power to transform their countries into pro-

---

* Railroads are an interesting example. In the beginning the
British considered the railroad as a special kind of road—that
is, every user of the road had to take care of his own carriage.
The result was that about 1850 an innumerable amount of non-
standardized carriages owned by private entrepreneurs used the
British railroads. In other countries the railroad companies
started immediately to offer *transport space*, not only *transport facilities.*

gressive ones. Resoluteness and political power were preconditions for success because the development process was, from a social point of view, ruthless.*

In the last chapter we saw that without industrialization an increase in population will in the long run lead to a decrease in the land-man ratio. As soon as a process of industrialization sets in to stop this tendency, an agrarian surplus is needed in order to feed the industrial workers.

Hamberg[40] has pointed out that a government may promise the people land or bread but not both at the same time. Via a land reform the government may give the farmers a patch of land, which often happens today in newly created nations. But unfortunately such a policy is not conducive to efficient farm management, and hence not for the creation of the agrarian surplus necessary to feed industrial labor. The French revolution certainly had the result that the level of living in the countryside improved somewhat, but at the same time it proved detrimental to the agrarian surplus.† Presumably this was one of the reasons for the rather late start of French industrialization.

In England, however, the *enclosure movement* drove the small farmers from their land. The result of this was first of all that the industrial centers could dispose of cheap labor and secondly that the agrarian surplus increased, because agrarian consumption on big farms is relatively low as compared with small farms.

But also the rapid increase in population sponsored the supply of cheap labor. In the beginning of the eighteenth century the population of England amounted to 5.8 million; it increased to 7.5 in 1781 and to 9.2 in 1801. It is highly likely that per capita income of the la-

* As far as we know, only in the United States was the situation different. A huge influx of foreign capital, a very favorable land-man ratio, and a favorable ratio of active to total population (due to immigration) were stimulating factors unknown in other countries.

† It is sufficiently known that the Soviets had the greatest difficulty in laying hands on the agrarian surplus.

boring poor—the normal appellation of the laborers in those days—remained constant or perhaps even declined during the eighteenth century, but because entrepreneurial incomes increased it is probable that income distribution became more unequal. Although no precise figures are known, Phyllis Deane mentions King's estimate for 1688 that the richest 8 per cent of the English families received 37 per cent of the national income, whereas Colquhoun estimated for 1803 that the same percentage received 43 per cent.[41] Incomes of skilled labor may have increased, but the small farmers driven from their land by the enclosures were unskilled laborers and their wages lagged behind the increasing price level.[42]

We think that this increase in the inequality of income distribution is one of the attendant circumstances of economic development.* The explanation is rather simple: agrarian communities have a much greater social homogeneity and therefore a much more equal income distribution than industrial centers, where the possibilities of job diversification and hence of income differentials are far greater. The few Pareto coefficients for rural and urban areas in Table 5.4 indicate these

Table 5.4

PARETO COEFFICIENTS IN RURAL AND URBAN AREAS[43]

Country	Year	Rural Area	Urban Area
Germany	1894	1.86	1.38
	1902	1.84	1.36
Canada	1944	2.44	1.69/1.38
India	1929	1.68	1.33
	1949	1.71	1.19

differentials. But because industrialization goes hand in hand with urbanization, this means that more and more people will live under conditions of greater ine-

* Of course this does not mean that the average income also deteriorates.

quality.* We may assume, therefore, that as a result of economic development the distribution of income first of all becomes more unequal (Table 5.5). From this table

Table 5.5

LONG-TERM CHANGES IN PARETO COEFFICIENTS[44]

Year	England	Germany (*Prussia*)
1850	1.47	1.89
1880	1.41	1.58
1913	1.31	1.56
1930	1.61	1.78
1960	2.11	2.00

we can see that Prussia, about 1850 a largely agrarian country, had a much greater equality of income distribution than England, in those days already "the workshop of the world." In both countries the inequality increased until 1913. After World War I the tendency changed completely: income distribution became more equal.† This might be due to the *general* increase in education which had a greater impact on the increase of lower income than on higher.

Economists like Ricardo, Mill, and Marx who studied the economic conditions of England in the first part of the nineteenth century thought that an increasing income inequality was inherent in capitalism. They did not and could not see that the process is an essential part of economic development, but not of capitalism as such. Every economy aiming at rapid accumulation of capital in order to increase future production must keep the level of consumption low. Countries like England, Japan, and the Soviet Union which went through this process

* Although they are living at the same time at a higher average income than those who remained in the rural areas.

† These tendencies are even much stronger because the Pareto coefficients are computed before tax, and we have seen that direct taxation increased (in the relative as well as in the absolute sense) when per capita income goes up.

with little or no capital imports will feel this pressure even more strongly than countries where capital formation is partly financed out of foreign savings—i.e., through capital imports. But even if part of the economic development is financed from foreign resources, the main burden of accumulation has to be carried by the country itself.

We thus have seen that from the beginning of the seventeenth century a wood shortage jeopardized the British economy. This led to a strong tendency to substitute coal for wood. But this necessitated fundamental technological changes and a complete change in the system of transportation. It took more than 150 years before these problems were solved, but at the end of this period man had changed his environment. Man had understood that, as soon as he no longer considered his actual living conditions as inevitable, rational action could improve his situation. From that time onward an important part of Western culture concentrated on this improvement.

THE CASE OF JAPAN

Although in England an endogenous factor—the wood shortage—gave momentum to economic development, in Japan it was an exogenous factor—i.e., the increasing fear of foreign political interference, that achieved the same result. During the Tokugawa period (1603-1867) Japan had followed a policy of isolation and cultural consolidation. From the end of the eighteenth century several attempts were made by Western powers to open diplomatic and trade relations with Japan, mainly because these powers needed fueling ports. In 1853-54 Commodore Perry of the United States Navy forced the Japanese to open commercial relations; an example followed in due course by the other big powers. The opposition of the Tokugawa regime feared that Japan at that moment was facing China's fate.[45] This exogenous challenge led to the Restoration of the Emperor: the Meiji dynasty (1868), and to the creation of a highly centralized, rather authoritarian but also rather efficient government.

We have to add here that at the moment of the Restoration Japan was very weak but it had the enormous luck that the Big Powers could not agree on the partition of Japan: while France supported the feudal Tokugawa government, Britain was in favor of the new Meiji dynasty.[46] Without this controversy Japan would probably have been colonized, which at that time, would definitely not have helped its economic development.[47] But one might also argue, paradoxically enough, that the Big Powers were not particularly interested in Japan because its resources were so poor. About 1860 the per capita income certainly did not surpass $45 (in 1952-54 prices). The paradox is that Japan seems to have developed because it was poor to begin with.

In the 1860s lower-rank officers, the *samurai,* understood that Western technology not only brought wealth, but also—from an international point of view—power. They also realized that under the existing feudal system Japan would never rise to be a modern state.[48] They were aware that Japan needed industrialization in order to support a big army and navy. They sponsored the Restoration of the Emperor, whose power surpassed anything known in the West.*

The *samurai* swept away everything that might block their stride towards a modern state and a modern economy,[49] but at the same time they endeavored to conserve as much as they could for the traditional Japanese values, so that they would never "lose their soul." [50]

We have seen that in Britain no conscious governmental development policy ever existed, but in Japan development was heavily sponsored by the Government. This policy however was far from dogmatic: it aimed only at making the nation strong; the Government did not particularly care who was going to do the job. In the

---

* A rich country, a strong army (fukoku kyohei) became the slogan of the new dynasty.

beginning—i.e., after 1870—the Government, with the aid of foreign experts, launched a great many industrial enterprises. About 1880 most of these state enterprises turned out to be nonprofitable and the Government then sold them at rather low prices to the Zaibatsu (a group of eight rich Japanese families), with the ultimate intention of encouraging private initiative.

Thus far Japanese and British development have nothing in common, but we shall see hereafter that conformity was greater than one would assume at first sight.

We have seen that an increase in per capita income requires an increase in the rate of investment and/or a decrease in the capital coefficient (4.8). For England during the period of economic development, no reliable statistical material is available. We therefore have passed by this question in silence so far, but for Japan much more data are at our disposal. Japan's industrial development—and especially the textile industry—started at a very low capital intensity. About 1910 in English spinning mills 1,000 spindles were handled by six laborers, as against 10 in Germany and 50 in Japan.[51] The last figure is in harmony with Ranis' findings that in the period 1906-10 one laborer handled 20 spindles.[52] Although Ranis does not give his data in money terms, it seems permissible to use changes in the ratio between the number of spindles and the production in *kan* (1 kan = 3.75 kg) as a first approximation of the changes in the capital coefficient (see Table 5.6). We see that the decrease in K/O during the period 1886-1900 was caused by the increase in labor productivity O/L and the decrease in capital intensity K/L. Particularly during the period 1886-95, labor input increased much faster than capital (spindle) input. Thus during that period the Japanese industrialists were able to employ more labor per unit of capital without lowering labor productivity. This certainly required first-class managerial capacities. Because the textile industry in those days was Japan's most important industry,[53] we

Table 5.6

CAPITAL INTENSITY, LABOR PRODUCTIVITY AND
CAPITAL COEFFICIENT IN JAPANESE TEXTILE
INDUSTRY (1886-1921)

Year	Average Number of Spindles used in Production per Day (K)	Average Amount of Laborers (L)	Production per Day (in kan), (O)	$\frac{K}{L}$	$\frac{O}{L}$	$\frac{K}{O}$
1886-90	129	6,000	6,600	21.5	1.10	19.5
1891-95	391	9,160	33,600	13.4	1.15	11.6
1896-1900	961	57,860	85,700	16.6	1.48	11.3
1901-05	1,296	66,840	103,800	19.6	1.57	12.5
1906-10	1,613	80,850	133,000	20.0	1.65	12.1
1911-15	2,331	109,230	204,000	21.3	1.87	11.4
1916-21	3,619	150,570	261,500	24.0	1.74	13.8

may consider that industry as representative of the total.[54]

During that period not only was existing machinery more fully exploited, but the capital coefficient declined too, through the introduction of more shifts. Ranis points out that working more shifts has the advantage of accelerating capital amortization so that machinery can be replaced sooner by better equipment.

The gradual increase of K/L after 1891-95 presumably indicates that in spite of the high labor intensity the rationalization of production set in rather early.* This is in complete accordance with our theoretical consideration that a poor country by using its existing capital in the most efficient manner, must be able to finance (part of) its capital formation.

* In the nineteenth century 75 laborers were used per 1,000 spindles against 50 in 1906-10.

The low-capital coefficient in Japanese industrial production during the period of economic development
may be also due to the important role of small industry,
because the capital coefficient in small industry is lower
than in the bigger firms.[55]

Table 5.7

PERCENTAGE DISTRIBUTION OF PRODUCTION BETWEEN
SMALL AND LARGE INDUSTRIES[56]

Year	Small Industry	Large Industry
1878	67.5	32.5
1895	59.5	40.5
1920	33.3	67.7
1930	31.3	68.7

Labor has been used during the Japanese process of
economic development in a very efficient manner. For
centuries the population had remained practically constant and perhaps the land-man ratio did not change
during a millennium.[57] However, after the Restoration
population increased rapidly (about 1.2 per cent per
annum), and the augmentation of the economically active population found employment, for the greatest part,
in the secondary and tertiary sector.

In the beginning, agrarian population still increased,
but at the turn of the century an absolute decrease set
in. During the period 1879-1928 the contribution to
national income of the agrarian sector declined from
63.9 to 21.2 per cent, whereas the contribution of the
secondary increased from 10.5 to 27.0 per cent and of
the tertiary from 25.6 to 51.8 per cent.[58]

The relative decline of the importance of the agrarian
sector and the rapid progress in industrial production
both found their reflection in the structural changes in the
import-export pattern during the second half of the nineteenth century. Whereas in 1868-72 tea exports ac-
counted for 24.5 per cent of the total exports and finished manufactures for 1.9 per cent, the situation was
exactly reversed at the end of the century. In 1890-

Table 5.8

DISTRIBUTION OF THE ECONOMICALLY ACTIVE
POPULATION (MILLIONS)[59]

Period	Total Population	Economically Active Population	In Primary Sector	In Secondary Sector	In Tertiary Sector
1878-82	35.9	19.5	16.1	1.1	2.4
1883-87	37.9	21.2	16.8	1.6	2.9
1888-92	40.4	22.6	17.2	2.0	3.4
1893-97	42.3	23.8	17.4	2.5	4.0
1898-02	44.9	24.8	17.3	2.9	4.5
1903-07	47.5	25.6	17.0	3.4	5.2
1908-12	51.0	26.2	16.5	3.9	5.8
1913-17	54.9	26.5	15.7	4.4	6.5
1918-22	58.0	27.1	14.9	4.6	7.6
1923-27	60.6	28.4	14.8	4.9	8.8

1902 tea exports contributed 4.1 per cent only to total exports, and finished manufactures had risen to 26.7 per cent.[60]

K. Akamatsu[61] supposes that economic development can be characterized by this import-production-export relation. Consumer goods show an increase first in imports, then in production, and last of all in exports. With a certain time lag, capital goods follow with the same pattern. Data on the Japanese import-export relation more or less confirm this thesis (Table 5.9). Akamatsu in this connection speaks of the flying-geese pattern,* because wild geese fly in overlapping shape like that of Fig. 5.2. It certainly takes a tradition of many centuries in fine drawing to detect such a pattern in the graph, but one has to admit it gives a nice image of rapid economic development.

From the beginning, small enterprise has played an important role in Japanese economic development. This is significant because in many of the low-income countries an argument against small enterprise is the low

* *Gankokeitai* in Japanese.

Table 5.9

CHANGES IN THE COMMODITY COMPOSITION OF THE
JAPANESE FOREIGN TRADE
(IN PER CENT OF TOTAL)[62]

Commodity	Imports		Exports	
	1868-72	1898-1902	1868-72	1898-1902
Food	29.0	22.9	32.2	12.0
Raw material	4.1	31.4	23.2	11.3
Total	33.1	54.3	55.4	23.3
Semimanufactured raw material	20.2	16.3	40.8	47.8
Finished manufactures	44.5	28.0	1.9	26.7
Total	64.7	44.3	42.7	74.5

rate of savings in the small, labor-intensive industries.*

However, in Japan the rate of saving was very high; during the period 1906-35 it amounted to 20.5 per cent.[63] Frugality was not only specially underlined in the family code of the Mitsui, but all entrepreneurs were very thrifty.[64] Strangely enough, however, the lower-

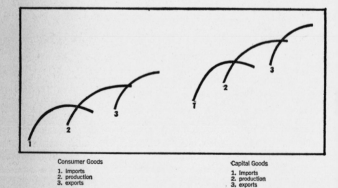

Consumer Goods
1. imports
2. production
3. exports

Capital Goods
1. imports
2. production
3. exports

FIG. 5.2   Flying-geese pattern of economic development

* Also, taxation of the big enterprise is easier for the Government than of a great many small plants.

income brackets in Japan contributed considerably to the savings. If we assume that the bank deposits reflect the savings of the higher-income brackets, and postal savings those of the lower ones, Table 5.10 dem-

Table 5.10
BANK DEPOSITS AND DEPOSITS AT JAPANESE POST OFFICE SAVINGS BANKS[65]

Year	Bank Deposits	Post Office Savings Banks	Total
1875	1.0	0.0	1.0
1880	7.3	0.7	8.0
1885	11.4	9.1	20.5
1890	31.8	21.3	53.1

onstrates the impressive contribution of the latter. However, the most important form of savings were the involuntary (forced) savings, because the increase in real wages lagged behind the increase in labor productivity, as expressed in the per capita income in the secondary sector.[66]

Table 5.11
REAL WAGES AND LABOR PRODUCTIVITY IN JAPANESE INDUSTRY (1878-82 = 100)[67]

Period	Per Capita Income in the Secondary Sector (Labor Productivity)	Real Wages in the Secondary Sector
1878-82	100	100
1883-87	126	111
1888-92	138	108
1893-97	157	117
1898-02	196	139
1903-07	173	136
1908-12	194	148
1913-17	239	148
1918-22	282	214
1923-27	338	289
1928-32	499	395
1933-37	576	350
1938-42	677	320

The fundamental choice[68] between less consumption with rapid progress and more consumption with less progress was made unequivocally in favor of the former. The result was a very low level of consumption during the period of economic development,* but afterwards the percentage increase was greater than that in other countries.

Table 5.12
INDEX OF REAL WAGES (1873-77 = 100)[69]

Period	Japan	Sweden	Great Britain	United States
1873-77	100	100	100	100
1893-97	125	150	140	139
1913-17	158	171	131	136
1933-37	373	246	187	181

Although during the period of industrial development labor was heavily exploited in Japan, the main burden of forced savings was carried by the farmers. This certainly was not done with great enthusiasm, as is proved by the 190 peasant revolts during the period 1868-78, against 157 between 1845 and 1868.

Immediately after the Restoration, tax reforms were introduced with the final result that agriculture had to pay the lion's share of taxation. The antiquated feudal tax levied on the *yield* of the land was transformed into a tax on the value of the land.[70] The introduction of this

Table 5.13
YIELD OF JAPANESE LAND TAX (IN 1,000 YEN)[71]

	Total Government Revenue	Total Tax Revenue	Land Tax as Percentage of Total Tax Revenue
1868	33,039	3,157	63.7
1872	50,445	21,845	91.8
1876	69,482	59,194	85.0

* One must remember that in 1880 the per capita income in Japan was not higher than $45.

land tax had a few important repercussions. The first, of course, was that the government knew in advance how much could be expected from the land tax. Because the land tax does not increase when the yield of the land improves it gives a strong impulse to agricultural productivity. Although the land tax was heavy the Japanese government did a lot to improve the agrarian situation. It furnished the necessary capital for agricultural enterprises, established experimental farms and agricultural colleges. The Government also published information bulletins in addition to the importation of foreign know-how, farm implements, and machinery in a well-designed program aimed at improving the technique of farming.

As long as the Government followed an inflationary policy, the peasant's tax burden was not too heavy, but after 1881 the new Finance Minister Matsukata followed a strong deflationary policy[72] with the result that many of the small farmers were not able to pay their taxes and had to sell their land.[73] Thus the final outcome was the same as that of the enclosure movement in Britain: agricultural laborers were forced to leave their land. Thus the supply of industrial labor increased and wages remained low.

This low wage level and hence the low level of consumption was of paramount importance for the economic development of Japan. Japan wanted to introduce Western technology as quickly as possible but, for fear of foreign political intervention, excluded foreign capital. During the period 1868-95 only two foreign loans were taken up (in 1870 and 1873). Together they did not amount to more than 3 per cent of the national income of that time.

Thus we can say that Japan financed, in a rather short period, the whole of its economic development out of its own resources. Many foreign experts were engaged but the government took care that they did not gain control over Japanese firms. The government stipulated, for example, that a state enterprise sold to a Japanese entrepreneur could engage foreign experts but could not have a foreigner as a partner.[74]

After the Chinese War, Japan obtained its capital imports on extremely favorable conditions: China had to pay its war indemnity in sterling in London.[75] This had a very favorable effect on the balance of payment as the indemnity equaled half the Japanese national income. As a result of this improvement in foreign assets Japan was able to introduce the gold standard in 1897. But during the first twenty-five years Japan financed its development from its own means, which resulted in a very low level of consumption. There is some truth in Nurkse's statement that Japan duplicated in those days everything from the West except for the level of consumption.[76]

The remark has so often been made that Japan copied everything from the West that a short digression on this topic seems necessary.

We have pointed out before that at the beginning of a process of a country's economic development stands the conviction of its elite that it must be possible to alter the environment. We have seen that in the case of England great technological problems had to be overcome before this became possible.

It is true that the Japanese could copy those techniques, but they understood immediately that they could not introduce them in the existing feudal society. They introduced Western techniques but they managed to adapt themselves to Western science and part of the Western outlook, without neglecting their own traditions and historically grown pattern of life. Theirs was the gift of assimilation and adaptation, not merely of imitation.

Furthermore, they showed both courage and a talent for compromise. Courage because they had to eliminate the feudal society with which they partly sacrificed the interests and properties of their own friends (the daimyos and samurais) from which classes most leaders of the Restoration sprang. They destroyed feudalism, but some of the old feudal leaders now became the leaders of modern society.[77]

Those who say that the Japanese "only" imitated Western technology completely fail to see that economic development means not only the introduction of new machinery, but the creation of a society in which these machines can function. By doing so the Japanese leaders were not much concerned about the prices paid by some groups of the population—e.g., the peasants. Their aim was the glory of Japan and to reach this aim individual sacrifices hardly counted.

CONCLUSION

It would have been possible to add the stories of other processes of economic development—e.g., of Sweden, West Germany, and the Soviet Union. They would have been different stories but the plot would have been practically the same.

In all we would find that man at a certain moment became aware of the necessity and the possibility of altering his environment; man became convinced that he could adapt society to fundamentally new conditions. It is this process of adaptation that we call economic development.

Because all traditional societies are agrarian economies, first of all a settlement with agrarian interests has to take place. The story in Britain, Japan and the Soviet Union is different, but the pattern of events is the same: productivity in agriculture increased and agrarian employment decreased, first relatively and later on also absolutely. Everywhere this has been a harsh process because rural interests resisted to the bitter end.*

The relative decline in agrarian employment goes hand in hand with the increase in industrial employment.

---

* The Japanese peasants' revolts, for example, were reactionary in character. We may add here that today agrarian pressure groups are the greatest stumbling block in the modernization of the European Market.

This in all cases called for fundamental improvements in management, but it also demanded a rapid accumulation of capital.

In all successful processes of economic development the fundamental choice between more consumption and more capital formation was decided in favor of the latter.

It goes without saying that such a policy found little response from the broad masses of the population. In the short run it was certainly detrimental to agrarian as well as to labor interests. In the long run, however, it led to a considerable increase in the level of living of the laborers.

NOTES

1. E. M. Forster, *Aspects of the Novel* (1927; Penguin edition 1962); G. M. Meier and R. E. Baldwin, in *Economic Development* (1957, p. 15), mention this distinction.

2. E. M. Forster, *op. cit.*, p. 35.

3. *Ibid.*, p. 93.

4. G. M. Meier and R. E. Baldwin, *op. cit.*, p. 119.

5. Compare D. C McClelland, *The Achieving Society* (1961), p. 423.

6. E. Lundberg describes in *Produktivitet och räntabilitet* (pp. 130-133) that in Horndal, one of the iron works of the Fagersta concern in Sweden, no new investments were made during a period of fifteen years, but that during this period labor productivity in Horndal increased on the average with 2 per cent per annum, against a 4 per cent increase for the whole of this concern. Although part of the increase in productivity in Horndal was due to the replacement of old machinery, it is obvious that a part of the increase in productivity was *not* due to the increase in capital intensity.

7. For 1695-1744 compare P. Studensky, *The Income of Nations* (1958), p. 51. These data have been deflated with the average of the price index of consumer goods and of capital goods as published by Phyllis Deane, *The Implications of Early National Income Estimates for the Meas-*

urement of Long-term Economic Growth in the United Kingdom, Reprint Series No. 109, University of Cambridge, Department of Applied Economics, 1956, p. 36. For 1800-70, Phyllis Deane, *Contemporary Estimates of National Income in the Second Half of the 19th Century,* Reprint Series 144, 1958, p. 459. For 1875-84 to 1946-52 James P. Jefferys and Dorothy Walters, "National Income and Expenditure of the United Kingdom, 1870-1952," in *Income and Wealth,* Series V, 1955, p. 14.

8. King's estimates are reproduced in Phyllis Deane, Reprint 109.

9. Compare K. Mandelbaum, *op. cit.,* p. 4.

10. We may mention here also Max Weber's idea that the Protestant Ethic was decisive (*The Protestant Ethic and the Rise of Capitalism,* tr. Talcott Parsons, 1956). Today we know that elites with a different ethical background have also been the leaders of social innovation processes; compare E. E. Hagen, *On the Theory of Social Change* (1962), pp. 16, 298, 394; and D. C. McClelland, *The Achieving Society* (1961), p. 147.

11. E. de Vries, *Man in Rapid Social Change* (1961), p. 35.

12. Erich Fromm, *May Man Prevail?* (1963), p. 4.

13. Erich Fromm, *op. cit.,* p. 5.

14. *Ibid.,* p. 4.

15. E. E. Hagen, *op. cit.,* p. 298.

16. Compare D. C. McClelland, *op. cit.,* p. 392.

17. J. Clapham, *A Concise Economic History of Britain* (1951), p. 228.

18. W. Sombart, *op. cit.,* II, 2, p. 1146.

19. Charles Singer (ed.), *A History of Technology* (1957), Vol. III, p. 78.

20. *Ibid.,* p. 220 and Vol. IV, p. 371.

21. Charles Singer, *op. cit.,* Vol. III, pp. 78, 81.

22. H. O. Meredith, *Economic History of England,* 4th ed. (1939), p. 201.

23. Charles Singer, *op. cit.,* Vol. III, p. 80.

24. Charles Singer, *op. cit.,* Vol. IV, p. 107.

25. E. A. Pratt, *A History of Inland Transportation in England* (1912), p. 190.

26. E. A. Pratt, *op. cit.,* p. 67.

27. *Ibid.,* p. 68.

28. E. A. Pratt, *op. cit.*, p. 175; compare E. Meteyard, *The Life of Josiah Wedgwood* (1865), I, p. 10, and II, pp. 5, 9.

29. We have made use here of an unpublished paper of Z. Y. Hershlag, Institute of Social Studies, The Hague.

30. See P. N. Rosenstein-Rodan, "Notes on the Theory of the 'Big Push,'" Massachusetts Institute of Technology, CIS, March 1957.

31. Compare T. S. Ashton, *An Economic History of England* (1955), p. 89.

32. Adam Smith, *op. cit.*, I, XI, p. 1.

33. P. Mathias, "Industrial Revolution in Brewery," in *Explorations in Entrepreneurial History*, Vol. V, p. 213.

34. P. Mathias, "The Entrepreneur in Brewery, 1700-1830," in *Explorations in Entrepreneurial History*, Vol. X, p. 72.

35. Compare H. Duller, "Een nieuwe visie op de groei," in *Economisch-Statistische Berichten*, October 1963.

36. Compare D. C. McClelland, *op. cit.*, p. 143, where he indicates that in the first half of the eighteenth century the export market to America increased considerably but that British traders were not taking advantage of it.

37. J. Ortega y Gasset, *Meditación de la Aécnica*, (1957), p. 17.

38. Compare B. F. Hoselitz, "Entrepreneurship and Capital Formation in France and Britain Since 1700," in *Capital Formation and Economic Growth* (1955), p. 322.

39. D. C. McClelland, *op. cit.*, pp. 233, 236.

40. D. Hamberg, *Economic Growth and Instability* (1956), p. 130.

41. Phyllis Deane, Reprint Series 128, p. 168.

42. *Ibid.*

43. Compare Colin Clark, *op. cit.*, pp. 538-539; M. Mukherjee and A. K. Gosh, *Bulletin of the International Institute*, Vol. XXXVI, Part II.

44. Compare Colin Clark, *op. cit.*, pp. 538-539.

45. Compare S. S. Kuznets (ed.), *Economic Growth* (1955), p. 539. In the following pages we have used much material from an unpublished paper by Hisao Onoe on the economic development in Japan (Institute of Social Studies, The Hague). This explains also quotations from some Japanese sources.

46. K. Inoue, *Meiji Ishin* (1951), Chap. 3 and 4.

47. Most of the colonized countries got an unbalanced economic structure with some well developed agrarian sectors for export products amidst a traditional Society. (Compare H. Myint, "An Interpretation of Economic Backwardness," *Oxford Economic Papers,* June 1954, pp. 153-159.

48. Compare E. H. Norman, *Japan's Emergence as a Modern State,* 1940.

49. T. C. Smith, *Political Change and Industrial Development in Japan, 1868-1880* (1955), p. 101.

50. A. J. Toynbee, *The World and the West* (1953), p. 54.

51. Compare E. A. Heber, *Japanische Industriearbeit* (1912), p. 165.

52. G. Ranis, "The Capital-output Ratio in Japanese Economic Development," *Review of Economic Studies,* October 1958, p. 24.

53. According to E. P. Reubens in Kuznets (ed.), (*Economic Growth,* 1955, p. 194) in 1895, 56.2 per cent of industrial investment was made in textile industry.

54. In an unpublished paper on The Pattern of Japanese Long-term Economic Growth, K. Ohkawa came to the conclusion that the overall industrial capital coefficient decreased from 1888-92 to 1893-97 from 3.9 to 2.6.

55. Some data on India are available:

CAPITAL COEFFICIENTS IN VARIOUS TYPES OF INDUSTRY

Industry	Capital per Laborer in Rupees K	Production per Laborers in Rupees, O	$\frac{K}{O}$	Number of Laborers per 10,000 Rupees Invested Capital
Modern large enterprise	1.200	650	1.9	8
Small enterprise	300	200	1.5	33
Cottage industry, automatic looms	90	80	1.1	111
Cottage industry, hand looms	35	45	0.8	286

Compare P. S. Lokanathan, "Cottage Industry and the Plan," in *Eastern Economist,* July 23, 1943.

56. G. Ranis, "The Capital-Output Ratio," p. 26.

57. Ryoichi Ishii, *Population Pressure and Economic Life in Japan* (1937), p. 140.

58. K. Ohkawa, *The Growth Rate of the Japanese Economy Since 1878* (1957), p. 26.

59. Computation made by the Economic Research Institute of the Hitotsubashi University.

60. Miyohei Shinohara, *Economic Development and Foreign Trade in Prewar Japan,* paper for the Study Group of Economic History of East and Southeast Asia, July 1961, University of London.

61. Quoted by Shinohara.

62. Miyohei Shinohara, *op. cit.*

63. K. Ohkawa, *The Growth Rate of the Japanese Economy Since 1878* (1957), p. 172. According to Clark the rate of savings in Germany in the period 1897-1909 was 17 per cent, and Kuznets estimates American savings at 16 per cent for 1884-1894. But these are exceptions. Cf. Tinbergen, *Economic Policy: Principles and Design* (1956), p. 89, who considers 15 per cent as already very high in a free economy.

64. Compare Colin Clark, *op. cit.*, p. 624.

65. Compare *Asian Affairs,* Vol. I, June 1956, p. 145.

66. K. Ohkawa, *Nippon Keizai no Bunseki,* Vol. I, 1956, p. 247.

67. Computed from *Nippon Keizai no Bunseki,* Vol. I (1956), p. 247, and K. Ohkawa, *op. cit.*, p. 34.

68. Compare J. Tinbergen, *Economic Policy: Principles and Design* (1956), p. 87.

69. J. Tinbergen, *op. cit.*

70. Compare T. C. Smith, *Political Change and Industrial Development in Japan: Government Enterprise 1868-1880* (1955), p. 74.

71. The tax was fixed initially at 3 per cent, which seems to have amounted to about 13 per cent of the value of a normal crop. We have used here an unpublished paper of Z. Joueijati on land tax (Institute of Social Studies).

72. Compare the price index of rice: 1873 = 100, 1881 = 210, 1885 = 129, D. M. Morris, "The Problems of the Peasant Agriculturist in Meiji Japan, 1873-1885," *Far Eastern Quarterly,* May 1956, p. 360.

73. S. Ohe, "A Peasant Revolt against the Reform of the Land Tax in the early Meiji Period," *Shigaku-Zasshi,* July 1956, p. 2.

74. Y. Horie, "Some Notes on the Exclusion Policy of Foreign Capital in the Earlier Period of the Meiji Era,"

VVV Keizai-Ronso, January 1932, p. 109; compare R. Nurkse, *op. cit.,* p. 89.

75. E. P. Reubens, "Foreign Capital and Domestic Development in Japan," in Kuznets (ed.), *Economic Growth* (1955), p. 181.

76. R. Nurkse, *op. cit.,* p. 143.

77. We have used in this past part a seminar paper of L. Q. M. Jacquet, (Japan seminar, Institute of Social Studies, The Hague).

Chapter 6

ECONOMIC PROGRESS

In Chapter I we mentioned that the distinction between economic growth, development, and progress was made not only for the sake of classification but on methodological grounds as well. We have seen in Chapter 4 that economic growth can be described with rather simple models. Assuming a constant capital coefficient it is the rate of savings that determines the increase in national production. In Chapter 5 we demonstrated that it is not possible to describe economic development in a mathematical model, but we hope we have succeeded in detecting the "plot" of the story.

When we come to the subject of economic progress we are back again to economic theory, although economic theory is here somewhat more complicated than in the case of economic growth.

We have seen that technology remained more or less constant during the period of economic growth. However, this statement needs some clarification. A bird's eye view of man's history makes clear that in the last ten or twenty thousand years fundamental inventions have been occasionally made, to mention only fire, the wheel, the introduction of agriculture and of domestic animals, the waterwheel, etc. But we agree with Ortega y Gasset[1] that those inventions, fundamental as they certainly were, were completely accidental. For example, it is highly unlikely that "fundamental research" was made in inventing the lever; man had to stumble on the principle of the lever one day or another—although it may be more realistic to speak of millennia instead of days. The problem is perhaps not so much of explaining the first completely accidental use made of a lever, but the conscious repetition of the knowledge thus acquired.

Even at the beginning of the nineteenth century, when Ricardo thought that the natural tendency of profits to fall was happily checked at repeated intervals by improvements in machinery (see page 8), it was not a continuous flow of technical progress that he had in mind, but occasional inventions. To Ricardo, inventions were still unpredictable and he therefore did not link them, as Marx did half a century later,[2] with a theory of profit and of competition. According to Marx, entrepreneurs, in order to survive the competitive race, must continuously introduce improved techniques. But such a continuous flow of innovations[3] is possible only when technical inventions are made continuously.

Because innovations are nothing but the application of an invention in economic life, inventions are a precondition for innovations. And indeed in the nineteenth century we observe a tremendous increase in scientific knowledge and technical power.

The reason for this is that all inventions are combinations of previously existing devices.[4] The coexistence of physical objects constitutes a possibility of combination,[5] hence the greater their amount, the greater the possibility of a new combination. This explains why technical progress has been so slow for ages: as long as the amount of available tools was very small the possibilities of combinations were small as well.

If we suppose, as Ayres does, that tool combinations occur in the same fashion as that in which digits are combined in the mathematical theory of permutations, then the resulting series is progressive in the mathematical sense—a series in which each member is derived from each preceding member by the same operation.[6] Hence technical progress is constantly accelerated and more and more is accomplished in shorter and shorter periods.[7] I think therefore, that we are allowed to state that scientific knowledge and technical power advance according to the law and at the rate of an increasing geometric progression or logarithmic function.[8]

TECHNOLOGICAL PROGRESS AND
ECONOMIC THEORY

Only in recent times have attempts been made to incorporate technical progress into economic theory.* This is mainly due to the fact that it was hard to find a secure place for technical progress in a theory largely biased by a linear homogeneous production function.† Although the expression is certainly not used in traditional economic theory, it is easy to show that constant returns to scale were tacitly assumed. In a competitive system, all agents of production automatically find their optimal allocation and once this stage has been reached it is not possible to increase production through the enlargement of the existing plants but only by adding new ones.[9]

It also seems fundamental to economic reasoning to assume that under competitive conditions total production Y equals the sum of the marginal productivity of labor dY/dL multiplied by the number of units of labor L, plus the marginal productivity of capital dY/dK times the number of units of capital K, or, in a mathematical form,

$$Y = \frac{dY}{dL} \cdot L + \frac{dY}{dK} \cdot K$$

Dividing by Y gives

$$1 = \frac{dY}{dL} \cdot \frac{L}{Y} + \frac{dY}{dK} \cdot \frac{K}{Y}$$

But because $(dY/dL)\cdot(L/Y)$ is the elasticity of production with respect to labor $(= a)$, and $(dY/dK)\cdot(K/Y)$

---

* This does not mean that in the past economists did not deal with technical progress at all; their main concern was to find out how far improvements in technology effected employment.

† All linear homogeneous production functions $Y = f(L,K)$ have the following property: if L and K are taken n times as large, Y is also n times as large as before. Thus a linear homogeneous production function implies constant returns to scale.

is the elasticity of production with respect to capital ($= \beta$), we may also write:

$$1 = a + \beta$$

This means that if L becomes n times as large, Y becomes $\propto n$ times as large, and if K becomes n times as large, Y becomes βn times as large. Thus if both become n times as large, Y becomes n times as large as well.

It is therefore understandable that the linear homogeneous variant of the Cobb-Douglas production function[10]

$$Y = L^a K^{1-a}$$

became the time-hallowed favorite,[11] in spite of the fact that Douglas himself remarks[12] that his function eliminates progress or dynamic improvements in the quality of capital, labor and the industrial arts from industrial history.

It is easy to demonstrate the relationship between the Cobb-Douglas production function and the Harrod-Domar model. Since according to the Cobb-Douglas function

$$\frac{dY}{Y} = a \frac{dL}{L} + (1 - a) \frac{dK}{K}$$

and since with constant returns to scale the long-term equilibrium requires

$$\frac{dL}{L} = \frac{dK}{K}$$

and further since

$$dK = I = S = sY$$

and

$$\frac{Y}{K} = \frac{1}{k}$$

we may write, *so long as we assume that no further substitution of factors takes place:*[12]

$$\frac{dY}{Y} = a\frac{s}{k} + (1-a)\frac{s}{k}$$

or

$$\frac{dY}{Y} = \frac{s}{k}$$

We have seen on page 81 that according to the Harrod-Domar model, labor productivity can increase only when capital intensity (K/L) increases proportionally—hence when the marginal productivity of capital goes down. The Cobb-Douglas production function allows for, but allows only for, changes in the combination of labor and capital along the same isoquant, hence more labor and less capital, or more capital and less labor to produce the same amount of output.

Today most economists will agree that moving along the same isoquant is an excellent exercise in a graduate course in economics, but that it does not tell us much about actual economic life. We have already seen that Schumpeter defines an innovation as the setting of a new production function, and Solow uses the phrase "technical change" as a shorthand expression for *any kind of shift* in the production function.[13]

A shift in the production function means that output per unit of input (be it of labor, capital, or both) increases, as a result of the improvement in the *quality* of labor, capital, or both.*

One possibility of introducing this technical progress in the production function is by expressing this improvement in quality in quantitative terms—i.e., if the quantity of labor increases by 1 per cent and labor productivity increases by 1 per cent as well, one can say that labor input increases by 2 per cent. If we call the percentage increase in labor productivity T_l and the percentage increase in capital productivity T_k, we can write the production function thus:

---

* This can, of course, be the result of improvements in the organization.

$$\frac{dY}{Y} = a \left(\frac{dL}{L} + T_l \right) + (1 - a) \left(\frac{dK}{K} + T_k \right)$$

But this equation does not show us the essence of technical progress because it is, after all, the *quality* and not the *quantity* of labor that increases. Because the quality of labor and of capital increases continuously (i.e., because output per unit of input increases continuously) it seems much more realistic to describe this situation by increasing the elasticity of production with respect to labor with ϵ_l and the elasticity of production with respect to capital with ϵ_k:

$$\frac{dY}{Y} = (a + \epsilon_l) \frac{dL}{L} + (1 - a + \epsilon_k) \frac{dK}{K}$$

Thus the contribution of technical progress to labor productivity per unit of time is ϵ_l and to capital productivity is ϵ_k. This method has been followed by M. M. Al-Homssi,[14] although he attributes the increase in productivity entirely to the increase in the efficiency of capital. Starting from the oft-quoted statistical findings for industrialized countries,

$$Y = L^{3/4} K^{1/4}$$

he estimates for the periods 1930-38 and 1948-55 for Great Britain, France, and Germany

$$Y = L^{3/4} K^{1/3}$$

That is, Al-Homssi estimates that for the said periods and the said countries the sum of the two elasticities is 1.08, and the annual contribution of technical progress to productivity is $(d/dt) (K^{0.08})$. However, doubt may arise as to whether it is realistic to impute the increase in efficiency to capital only. We have already mentioned on page 104 the *Horndal effect*—i.e., the autonomous increase in labor productivity as a result of learning by experience, improvements of habits, and techniques of work—in organization, the increase in efficiency due to better education, etc.[15] So far as the latter is concerned, E. F. Denison[16] has drawn attention to the fact that in

1960 the U.S. labor force had spent 2½ times as many days in school as its 1910 counterpart. Denison estimates that these improvements in education contributed 23 per cent of the total growth of national product during the said period.[17]

This means, therefore, that we have to impute part of the increase in productivity directly to labor.

Thus technical progress means that an increase in output is accompanied by a less than proportional increase in inputs. Three possibilities can be distinguished:

(*a*) All inputs show the same percentage quantitative increase, but the percentage in output is greater (neutral technical progress).

(*b*) The percentage quantitative increase in $L < K$, and the percentage increase in output is equal to or greater than the percentage increase in K (laborsaving technical progress).

(*c*) The percentage quantitative increase in $K < L$, and the percentage increase in output is equal to, or greater than the percentage increase in L (capital-saving technical progress).

The foregoing means that if under conditions of constant returns to scale labor and capital increase with the same percentage, but at the same time, due to technical progress, the quality of labor and capital improves as well, the percentage increase in production is greater than the quantitative percentage increase in inputs; that is, one observes (due to technical progress) the effect of increasing returns to scale.

However, thus far it seems to have been impossible, due to the lack of statistical data, to measure ϵ_l and ϵ_k separately. Therefore

$$\epsilon_l \frac{dL}{L} + \epsilon_k \frac{dK}{K} = \epsilon$$

is rather often computed as a residual:

$$\epsilon = \frac{dY}{Y} - \left(0.75 \frac{dL}{L} + 0.25 \frac{dK}{K} \right)$$

and the general form of the increase in national income is then written:

$$\frac{dY}{Y} = \epsilon + a\frac{dL}{L} + (1 - a)\frac{dK}{K}$$

But the equation shows that when L and K both increase by 1 per cent, Y increases by more than 1 per cent. And although we are not yet able to distinguish between ϵ_l and ϵ_k, I nevertheless think that a formula

$$\frac{dY}{Y} = (a + \epsilon_l)\frac{dL}{L} + (1 - a + \epsilon_k)\frac{dK}{K}$$

gives us a better insight into what technical progress really means, because we can draw a rather interesting theoretical conclusion from this last equation. We have already seen that under pure competition the sum of the marginal product of labor times the number of labor units, plus the marginal product of capital, multiplied by the number of capital units equals total production, and that therefore the sum of the two elasticities must be equal to 1.[18] Hence only one conclusion is possible: pure competition is incompatible with technical progress.

TECHNOLOGICAL PROGRESS:
A SOCIAL PHENOMENON

We assume that once the period of economic development is finished and economic progress sets in, technical progress becomes a *social* phenomenon. Whereas Schumpeter thought that innovations (i.e., shifts in the production function) are introduced by men of genius, by creative entrepreneurs,[19] we think that those individual innovators played an important role during the period of economic development but that the period of economic progress is characterized by the institutionalization of technical progress. The genius, the great inventor, or the great entrepreneur of earlier times has vanished in the anonymity of the modern laboratory or

board of directors. It is a long time since the picture of
the entrepreneur was used as a trademark* and modern
management experts even consider the "great man"
image a possible detriment to the continuity of a firm.[20]
Although Schumpeter's thesis that creative entrepreneurs
cannot be foreseen remains of course true, it seems to
have lost its actuality.[21]

It is for this reason that we may define economic
progress as an epoch in which technical progress and
economic innovations take place continuously. It is no
longer the huge, abrupt shifts in the production function that characterize economic change, but the perpetual flow of marginal shifts. It is exactly for this reason
that we find in the advanced economies rather constant
numerical values for ϵ, varying between 0.010 and
0.015. For the long-term model we wish to develop be-
low we assume a value of 0.012.

So far as dL/L is concerned, it seems realistic to assume an increase of 0.012 per annum if we measure it
as the labor hours input. The percentage increase in
capital has certainly surpassed the percentage increase
in labor inputs in all advancing countries over the past
100 years. We make a very modest guess by assuming
that $dK/K = 0.02$. In order to understand what this
would imply, simply imagine a country where the capital coefficient is 3 and the rate of savings[22] is 6. Applying these numerical data to the formula

$$\frac{dY}{Y} = \epsilon + a\frac{dL}{L} + (1 - x)\frac{dK}{K}$$

gives

$$2.6 = 1.2 + (0.75 \times 1.2) + (0.25 \times 2)$$

If in Great Britain—and these data are realistic approximations for that country in the period 1800-1960

---

* King Gillette (1855-1932) is still depicted on the Gillette
Blue Blade package, although not on the newer stainless-steel
blade package.

—the rate of savings and hence the percentage increase in capital doubles, the percentage increase in national income becomes

$$3.1 = 1.2 + (0.75 \times 1.2) + (0.25 \times 4)$$

Hence as a result of doubling the rate of savings the percentage increase in national income will go from 2.6 to 3.1—i.e., an increase of 20 per cent; a meager reward for what is, after all, a revolution in the speed of capital accumulation.[23] And although it is true that we now entirely neglect the fact that capital formation is also a vehicle for carrying technical change into effect, we think nevertheless that we can describe economic progress much better in terms of *technical progress,* than in terms of speeding up capital accumulation. But it follows from page 139 that the precondition for a continuous flow of new combinations is the existence of a certain minimum amount of possibilities for combinations. It is for this reason that during the first stages of economic development capital formation is of much more importance than in later stages of economic progress.

ECONOMIC PROGRESS AND
INCOME DISTRIBUTION

We have seen on page 119 that it seems realistic to assume that during the epoch of economic progress the income distribution became more unequal at first, and became more equal in a later stage. We think that it is possible to explain this general tendency in a rather simple progress model.

We start with the assumption that labor productivity under economic progress increases at a constant rate, hence

$$P = P_0 e^{\epsilon_t}$$

where P ($= Y/L$) is the labor productivity and ϵ the average amount percentage increase in labor productivity. Because in the United Kingdom over the last 200 years per capita income has increased at an average rate of 1.2 per cent,* we assume that

$$P = P_0 e^{1.2t}$$

It seems realistic to assume that when labor productivity increases, the real wage level will increase also. How great the proportion is will depend on the bargaining power of the trade unions. We assume that at the first stage of economic progress the proportion will be lower than in later stages, when the influence of the unions will be greater. It is not impossible that at a certain stage they will get even more than the increase in labor productivity. Here we assume that the wage level V increases with a constant percentage a of the increase in labor productivity. Hence

$$\frac{dV}{dt} = a\,(P - V)$$

Let us call the remainder

$$\frac{dP}{dt} - (P - V)$$

the *surplus*. It does not matter in our model who gets this surplus, it may go to private innovators or to the government. The only thing that matters is that labor does not harvest all the fruits of the increase in labor productivity, and that therefore a surplus is available to finance additional capital formation. We have already demonstrated that economic progress is incompatible with pure competition where labor earns its marginal productivity. One of the reasons seems to be that in a progressing economy the *ex ante* remuneration of the factors of production is always lower than the *ex post* imputations. We can thus define the surplus as the difference between *ex post* imputation and *ex ante* remuneration.[24] This is in complete harmony with F. H. Knight's statement that entrepreneurs are cautious in their com-

* Table 2.4 demonstrates that this is a conservative estimate.

petition and do not let the price of the factors of production to their full theoretical value,[25] i.e., the imputation *ex post*.

We thus have introduced a time lag in the system of remuneration, and we think that this is a realistic assumption in a progressing economy where productivity increases continually and wages are adapted occasionally.

In order to understand what will happen in an economy when a continuous increase in labor productivity sets in, we take as a point of departure the Ricardian long-term equilibrium situation. According to Ricardo, in such an equilibrium situation no technical progress occurs, profits have disappeared, and the national income is divided between wages and rent. This could also be a rather good first approximation of an economy in which the largest proportion of the labor force is employed in agriculture. We introduce the following symbols:

Y = total value of production,
W = total wage bill
R = rent of land
S = surplus: $Y - W - R$, in our initial stage, (1)
thus equal to zero
L = labor force

$$P = \frac{Y}{L} = \text{gross productivity*} \qquad (2)$$

$$Q = \frac{Y - R}{L} = P - \frac{R}{L} = \text{net productivity} \qquad (3)$$

$$V = \frac{W}{L} = \text{wage rate} \qquad (4)$$

Share in total income of:

* Note that our original definitions have changed somewhat here; those who have no special interest in mathematics should continue on page 152 where the outcome of the model is discussed.

$$\text{Wages } = w = \frac{W}{Y} \tag{5}$$

$$\text{Surplus } = s = \frac{S}{Y} \tag{6}$$

$$\text{Rents } = r = \frac{R}{Y} \tag{7}$$

Since in the initial stage $S_0 = 0$, therefore $r_0 + w_0 = 1$. How do W, S, and r change during the process of economic progress?

We have seen in Chapter 5 that long after the period of economic development was over the situation of the laborers remained rather miserable. Many historians assume, for example, that the situation of the "laboring poor" in England was worse in 1850 than in 1750. As per capita income rose considerably during this period, it is highly likely that the income distribution worsened continuously. Our model does not do justice to these tendencies because we assume that from the very beginning a certain percentage of the increase in labor productivity was discounted in the wage level. However, it is highly likely that in the beginning the real wage level remained constant—that is, the whole increase in labor productivity went to the surplus.

We assume here however, that from the beginning the percentage increase in the wage level was proportional to the percentage increase in net labor productivity.

$$\frac{dV}{dt} = a\,(Q - V) \tag{8}$$

That is, we assume that from the very beginning of the increase in labor productivity the trade unions have been able to impute part of this increase to wages. We assume that the proportion remains constant, or

$$P = P_0 e^{\epsilon t} \tag{9}$$

Further we assume that labor hours also increased at a constant rate.

$$L = L_0 e^{\gamma t} \qquad (10)$$

To round off our model we need a fourth equation, and have taken into consideration that during a process of economic progress the quantitative importance of rent declined continuously. As a first approximation we assumed that the absolute level of rent income remained constant, hence that the relative importance declined continuously, or

$$R = R_0 \qquad (11)$$

Equations (8) through (11) can now be solved in conjunction with the definitional eqs. (1) through (7) to give the development over time of the relative shares in total income of wages, surplus and rents. F. M. O'Carrol [26] shows that the equilibrium share of wages and the surplus are respectively $(a)/(a + \epsilon)$ and $(\epsilon)/(a + \epsilon)$ and that the share of rents tends to zero.

The quantities w and s do not, however, move steadily towards their equilibrium values. To obtain a concrete picture of the development with respect to time of these ratios, the expressions given above have been evaluated using numerical values of the parameters a, ϵ, γ, and of the initial share of wages W_0. We have indicated already that it is not unrealistic to assume for a long period that $\epsilon = 0.012$, and in this particular case we may assume that γ also happens to be 0.012. The value to be used for a cannot be based on direct observations, but it is possible to obtain an idea of its magnitude from the fact that under modern conditions, employees' remuneration in many of the more advanced industrial countries amounts to about 70 per cent of national income. This ratio is not quite identifiable with the quantity W used in this theoretical analysis, as the remaining 30 per cent of national income contains many other elements besides our surplus, in particular it includes labor earnings of independent workers. Therefore, as a first approximation $W = 0.7$, or

$$W = \frac{a}{a + \epsilon} = 0.7$$

Thus $a = 0.028$, from which follows

$$\frac{a\,(\epsilon + \gamma)}{(a - \gamma)\,(a + \epsilon)} = 1.05$$

$$\frac{\gamma}{a - \gamma} = 0.75$$

$$\frac{a}{a - \gamma} = 1.75$$

and further,

$$W = 0.70 + (1.05 - 0.75\,W_o)e^{-0.4t} - 1.75 r_0 e^{-0.024t}$$

With the aid of this last equation we are able to compute the relative share of W, R, and S over time. The outcome of the computation is given in Table 6.1. According to Ricardo, in the long-term equilibrium situation, profits have disappeared (hence: $s = 1 - r - w = 0$), w receives about 75 per cent of national income, and r about 25 per cent. Those data were taken as a point of departure, and it was assumed that all at once labor productivity starts to increase by 1.2 per cent per unit of time, whereas the labor force increases by 1.2 per cent per unit of time.* Both assumptions are certainly not unrealistic for the United Kingdom at the beginning of the last century. Application of the last equation shows that during the first forty years the wage share decreased from 75 per cent to 63 per cent.

Thereafter a slow increase sets in and after about 150 years an equilibrium is reached when labor gets about 70 per cent and the surplus about 30 per cent.

If we assume that the model, in spite of all its assumptions and simplifications, can be used as a first approximative explanation of factual conditions, we are able to understand, for example, why many econo-

---

* The fact that both percentages are equal is completely coincidental.

Table 6.1

RELATIVE SHARE OF WAGES (w), RENT (r) AND
SURPLUS (s) IN NATIONAL INCOME OVER A PERIOD
OF 200 YEARS AFTER AN INCREASE OF LABOR
PRODUCTIVITY HAS SET IN

t	w	$r = 0.25\,e^{-0.24t}$	$s = I - r - w$
0	0.7500	0.2500	0.0000
2	0.7330	0.2383	0.0287
5	0.7107	0.2217	0.0676
8	0.6929	0.2063	0.1008
10	0.6826	0.1966	0.1208
15	0.6623	0.1744	0.1633
20	0.6483	0.1547	0.1970
25	0.6393	0.1372	0.2235
30	0.6339	0.1217	0.2444
35	0.6313	0.1079	0.2608
40	0.6309	0.0954	0.2734
45	0.6320	0.0849	0.2831
50	0.6342	0.0753	0.2905
60	0.6406	0.0592	0.3002
70	0.6481	0.0466	0.3053
80	0.6558	0.0366	0.3076
90	0.6629	0.0288	0.3083
100	0.6692	0.0224	0.3081
110	0.6748	0.0178	0.3074
120	0.6795	0.0140	0.3065
150	0.6893	0.0068	0.3039
200	0.6966	0.0020	0.3014

mists* in the first part of the past century thought that the wage share showed a tendency to decline, whereas about a hundred years later Paul Douglas defended the thesis that the wage share remains constant over time.

According to our model, both theories might be correct. However, they refer to different phases of the process of economic progress.

The numerical values of the parameters fit in rather well with Professor Verdoorn's empirical law of the increase in labor productivity. According to Verdoorn's law, the elasticity of the industrial labor productivity

* To mention only Carl Rodbertus-Jagetzow.

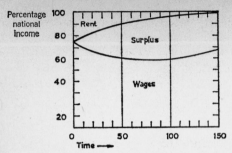

FIG. 6.1   Share of rent, surplus, and wages in national
income over a period of 150 years assuming
$a = 0.028$, $\epsilon = 0.212$, $\gamma = 0.012$, and $r_0 = 0.25$

with respect to the volume of production[27] is 0.5. Because in our example both labor productivity and labor
increased by 1.2 per cent, the total value of production
increased by 2.4 per cent. Hence the elasticity of the industrial labor productivity with respect to the volume of
production was 0.5.

Table 6.2

ELASTICITY OF LABOR PRODUCTIVITY WITH RESPECT
TO VOLUME OF PRODUCTION

| Country | Annual Percentage Increase | | Elasticity |
	Labor Productivity	Volume of Production	
Sweden			
1913–30	1.03	2.40	0.43
England			
1841–1907	0.98	2.40	0.41
1907–30	0.61	1.28	0.47
United States			
1869–99	2.31	5.61	0.42
1899–1950	1.80	3.85	0.47
Germany			
1882–1907	2.14	4.38	0.49
Japan			
1910–38	3.80	7.40	0.51

Although Verdoorn himself found somewhat different data for England, we reproduce here all his findings[28] because they demonstrate that 0.5 is a rather
realistic assumption.

NOTES

1. J. Ortega y Gasset, *op. cit.*, p. 77.
2. Compare B. Higgins, *Economic Development* (1959),
p. 115.
3. J. A. Schumpeter, *Business Cycles* (1939), Vol. I.,
p. 87. An innovation is the setting of a new production
function.
4. C. E. Ayres, *The Theory of Economic Progress*
(1944), p. 112.
5. C. E. Ayres, *op. cit.*, p. 115.
6. *Ibid.*, p. 119.
7. G. Sarton, *The Study of the History of Science*
(1936), p. 20, quoted by Ayres, *op. cit.*, p. 121.
8. A. Korzybski, *The Manhood of Humanity* (1922),
p. 20, quoted by Ayres, *op. cit.*, p. 120.
9. Compare P. A. Samuelson, "Abstract of a Theorem
Concerning Substitutability in Open Leontief Models," in
T. Koopmans, *Activity Analysis of Production and Allocation* (1951), p. 143.
10. Compare P. H. Douglas, *Theory of Wages* (1934),
Chap. 5.
11. R. M. Solow, "Investment and Technical Progress,"
in K. J. Arrow, S. Karlin and P. Suppes, *Mathematical
Methods in the Social Sciences* (1959), p. 90.
12. Compare A. E. Ott, "Production Functions, Technical Progress, and Economic Growth," in *International
Economic Papers* (1962), p. 110.
13. R. M. Solow, "Technical Change and the Aggregate
Production Function," in *Review of Economics and Statistics* (1957), p. 312.
14. M. M. Al-Homssi, *Economic Growth Potentials*
(1962), p. 26.
15. Compare R. M. Solow, *Capital Theory and the Rate
of Return* (1963), p. 42.
16. E. F. Denison, *The Sources of Economic Growth*

in the United States and the Alternatives Before Us (1962),
p. 73.

17. E. F. Denison, *op. cit.*, p. 267.

18. Compare E. H. Chamberlin, *The Theory of Monopolistic Competition* (1947), p. 182.

19. J. A. Schumpeter, "Economic Growth," in *Journal of Economic History*, Supp., VII, 1947, p. 8.

20. Peter Drucker, *The Practice of Management* (1954), p. 174, quotes an article in *Harper's Magazine* to the effect that if the top executive in a company gets a salary several times as large as the salaries paid to the Number Two, Three, and Four men, you can be pretty sure that the firm is badly managed. But if the salary levels of the four or five men at the head of the ladder are all close together, then the performance and morals of the entire management group is likely to be high.

21. J. A. Schumpeter, *op. cit.*

22. Compare, however, R. M. Solow, "Investment and Technical Progress," *op. cit.*, p. 97.

23. R. M. Solow, *op. cit.*, p. 97.

24. Compare S. Weintraub, *An Approach to the Theory of Income Distribution* (1958), p. 201.

25. See his article "Profit" in the *Encyclopaedia of the Social Sciences*, Vol. XII.

26. F. M. O'Carrol, "Income Distribution and Economic Development," in *Economic Planning*, editor L. J. Zimmerman (1963), p. 136.

27. P. J. Verdoorn, "Welke zijn de achtergronden en vooruitzichten van de economische integratie in Europa, en welke gevolgen zal deze integratie hebben, met name voor de welvaart in Nederland" *Vereniging voor de staathuishoudkunde* (1952), pp. 99, 128.

28. P. J. Verdoorn, *op. cit.*, p. 128. Some computations of E. F. Lari (Institute of Social Studies) have been added.

Chapter 7

THE WIDENING GAP

We have demonstrated that during the past one hundred years, the distribution of world income has become more and more unequal—that the gap between the rich and the poor countries has constantly increased. We have seen that this was partly due to the differences in the rates of saving in the rich and poor countries, and partly to the much greater technological progress in the industrial communities. However, we found as a more fundamental cause that in some parts of the world the capacity to respond to change, to induce change, and to accept change has been and still is much greater than in others. And we have also seen that a high propensity to accept innovations[1] is a precondition of economic progress.

It is often argued that, particularly during the past century, Western countries brought a great many innovations to their colonies, but that these innovations did not lead to self-sustained progress. On the contrary, they often resulted in a certain fossilization: one traditional society was exchanged for another, but no fundamental overall change in society took place. Haberler[3] even considers possible cases where these innovations might turn against the country. When, for instance (as a result of the introduction of plantations) exports and therefore imports also increase, this may destroy part of the domestic production and create (disguised) unemployment.*

Of course, according to the static equilibrium theory (with assumptions of both spontaneous and timeless adaptation), this increase will result either in such a reduction in factor remuneration that the domestic pro-

* As was, for example, the case with Indian cloth production.

duction can continue to compete, or in a shift in production activities. However, if wages are already close to the subsistence minimum, it is hard to see how they could drop.[4] But there would appear to be a still more important factor. It is characteristic of traditional societies that even when circumstances have so altered that they flagrantly conflict with the existing sociocultural structures, these societies still try blindly to continue with their former modes of living until they cannot cope with the situation any further (see page 107).

EXPORTS—AGRICULTURAL OR INDUSTRIAL

One gets the impression that this holds true particularly for those countries that have specialized in the export of one commodity. As Lamartine Yates has pointed out (Table 7.1), their number is still increasing.

According to the Ricardian theory of international trade, the optimal international division of labor is attained if all countries exploit their respective comparative advantages as much as possible, and hence when all countries export but a very limited amount of different commodities.

Unfortunately, real life, and international trade particularly, are not tending toward a long-term equilibrium. International economic relations are not only changing continuously, but they also occasionally show sudden huge shifts. In real-life, therefore, countries that have only one horse on which everything has been staked[6] are often in an awkward position.

One hundred and fifty years after Ricardo developed his theory of international trade we must come to the conclusion that those countries that have concentrated on agrarian production and agrarian exports, and normally on the export of one or two commodities, are in an inferior position compared with that of their trade partners who have concentrated on industrial production and on a wide variety of industrial export products.

One of the factors responsible for the widening of the

Table 7.1

LOW-INCOME COUNTRIES OBTAINING IN 1913 AND IN 1953 MORE THAN 50 PER CENT OF EXPORT RECEIPTS FROM ONE PRODUCT[5]

In Beverages		In Other Foods	
1913	1953	1913	1953
Brazil		Panama	
Colombia		Cuba	
El Salvador		Mauritius	
Guatemala		Nigeria	
Haiti		Siam	
	Angola	French West Africa	Honduras
Venezuela	Ghana	Costa Rica	Formosa
Nicaragua	French Cameroons	Indochina	Ecuador
Ecuador	Ethiopia	Burma	
		In Minerals	
		Bolivia	
		Chile	
In Agricultural Raw Materials			
Liberia	Sudan		Venezuela
Egypt	Pakistan		Iraq
	Uruguay		Saudi Arabia
			Bahrain-Kuwait-Qatar
			Belgian Congo
Finland			Northern Rhodesia

gap seems to have been the much more rapid increase in exports in the industrial countries. Two factors work against a rapid increase in exports by many of the exporters of agrarian commodities. In the first place, their export products show declining income elasticities of demand when per capita incomes in the importing countries go up. Because the rich countries show rather rapid increases in per capita incomes, their consumption of primary commodities (and hence their imports) from low-income countries lag more and more behind the increase in their incomes.*

According to Raoul Prebisch,[7] for every 1 per cent of

Table 7.2

INCOME ELASTICITIES IN VARIOUS PARTS OF THE WORLD[8]

Country	Sugar	Coffee	Cacao	Fibers	Calories
Southeast Asia	1.3	1.5	0.8	1.1	0.6
Japan	0.8	1.5	0.7	0.9	0.2
Mediterranean countries	0.8	1.0	0.5	0.8	0.2
E.E.C. countries	0.5	0.6	0.3	0.5	0.1
United States	0.0	0.3	0.1	0.0	−0.03

per capita increase of income in the United States, imports of primary goods tend to increase 0.6 per cent. He could have added that this impressive disparity between the increase in income and imports (of primary commodities) has a tendency to become greater when incomes become higher.[8] It therefore is highly likely that in the nineteenth century, when per capita incomes in the United States and in Western Europe were much lower than they are today, these disintegrating factors in world trade hardly existed. One might therefore conclude that during that period the Ricardian approach to international trade was a rather realistic one.

Today the tendency mentioned above not only holds

* This was stated a long time ago, so far as foodstuffs are concerned, in Engel's law.

true as far as foodstuffs are concerned. A similar tendency exists for minerals—steel, copper, lead and tin—that consumption expands less rapidly than general manufacturing activity,[9] because modern technology shows a tendency of using less raw material per unit of output.

The rapid technological improvements in the industrial countries have to be mentioned as a second factor. Especially when the prices of the export products from the low-income countries are high, the tendency in rich countries to replace them by synthetic products is given fresh impetus. Jute and rubber may be quoted here as examples.

A few words have to be added here on the Prebisch-Singer thesis[10] that the terms of trade* show a secular movement detrimental to the exporters of primary commodities.[11]

According to Prebisch, one might have expected that in the long run the prices of industrial products would have fallen relative to those of the primary products, due to the greater technical progress in the production of the former.[12] But in reality the reverse has taken place.

Prebisch's explanation is simple: in the industrialized countries (owing to the power of monopoly both on the commodity markets and on the labor market) incomes of entrepreneurs as well as of laborers have increased faster than productivity, whereas (owing to the fierce competition on the markets of primary commodities) the opposite holds true for nonindustrialized countries. For instance, the absence of strong trade unions in underdeveloped countries allowed the rise in productivity enjoyed by certain export sectors resulting from foreign investment to be reflected in lower prices, while the effective presence of these factors was not adequately reflected in falling prices in manufactured goods in the rich countries.[13]

* The terms of trade indicate the ratio between export and import price indexes; thus a favorable movement of the terms of trade is shown by a rising index.

Therefore, according to Singer, the industrialized countries have had the best of both worlds, both as consumers of primary commodities and as producers of manufactured articles, whereas the low-income countries have had the worst of both worlds, as consumers of manufactures and as producers of raw materials.[14]

TRENDS IN TOTAL EXPORT REVENUES

Although these factors may help to account for the widening gap, their importance should certainly not be exaggerated. If incomes indeed increase faster than productivity in rich countries and slower in poor countries, inflationary pressures in the former should be much greater than in the latter. But considerable doubt exists as to whether or not this is correct.[15] But we may also doubt whether it is useful to focus attention on the terms of trade. Prices of primary commodities may rapidly increase due to failures in harvests—as was for instance the case with cocoa in the postwar years[16]—but this was certainly not a favorable change.

It makes much more sense, therefore, to compare the trends in total export revenues of rich and poor countries than to digress on the terms of trade. And because the income elasticities of demand for many of the primary commodities show a long-term tendency to decline and to approach zero, we may expect in the long run that the exports of the producers of primary commodities, even with completely stable prices, will not grow much faster than the population increase in the rich countries—i.e., by not more than 2 per cent per annum.

We have to try first of all to find an explanation for the differences in the trends in total export revenues of rich and poor countries—first, because exports are one of the factors determining national income (and hence one of the factors explaining the increase in national income), and second because exports are of paramount

(1953 = 100)

Country	1950	1951	1952	1954	1955	1956	1957	1958	1959	1960	1961	1962
Netherlands	66	91	98	112	125	133	144	149	168	187	200	213
Sweden	75	120	106	107	117	131	144	141	149	173	185	197
Belgium-Luxembourg	73	117	108	102	123	140	141	135	146	167	174	191
Denmark	74	94	95	108	118	124	131	144	157	167	172	185
Malaya	133	210	130	102	102	148	142	137	118	183	164	164
Mexico	80	98	99	112	138	150	124	126	129	130	142	160
United Kingdom	85	101	101	104	113	123	129	124	130	139	144	148
Philippines	82	103	88	101	101	114	108	124	133	141	125	139
Cameroons	63	87	84	116	127	100	108	155	144	129	131	138
United States	65	95	96	96	99	121	132	113	111	130	133	136
Nigeria	73	97	104	120	106	108	103	109	132	137	139	136
Chile	69	91	110	98	116	133	112	95	121	120	124	130
Ghana	85	104	96	131	109	99	102	117	128	131	130	130
India	106	147	125	106	114	117	124	110	118	121	120	128
Australia	84	103	85	84	88	95	111	84	101	99	117	119
Ceylon	100	122	96	116	124	111	107	109	112	117	111	116
Argentina	104	105	63	91	83	84	87	88	90	96	86	108
United Republic	123	143	102	101	102	100	121	117	113	139	119	98
Turkey	66	79	92	85	79	77	87	62	90	81	88	96
Indonesia	95	154	92	103	113	110	114	94	111	100	93	80
Brazil	88	115	92	102	93	96	90	81	83	82	91	79
Colombia	66	77	79	110	97	101	86	77	79	78	73	78
Uruguay	94	87	77	92	68	78	47	51	36	48	65	57

importance for determining a country's capacity to import.)

Table 7.3 gives the export figures for twenty-three countries as published in the *Statistical Yearbook of the United Nations*. Index numbers have been devised for the 1950-62 exports (f.o.b.) in dollars, with 1953 as a basis.* Next the exponential trend for each individual country has been computed. By weighting the latter with the absolute amounts of exports, the trend for seven economic-geographic areas has been developed (Table 7.4, *T*). One sees immediately that total exports, and hence total import capacity, increased much more slowly in the low-income areas than in the higher-income areas.

But perhaps even more important than these numerical values of the trends are the average annual percentage deviations from the respective trends (Table 7.4, *F*). These turned out to be much greater in the poor countries than in the richer ones.

✓ This means that exports in low-income countries not only increase rather slowly, but also fluctuate rather heavily from year to year. We face here one of the most difficult elements in the process of economic development in low-income countries.

Development planning calls for an estimate of future imports of capital goods and raw materials, but when the import capacity is liable to heavy fluctuations, development planning means planning for balance of payments difficulties.

These huge fluctuations in export revenues may, however, be used also as an explanatory variable for the low numerical values of the trends in exports: the greater the uncertainty, the smaller the willingness of businessmen to venture in exports.

It is easy to understand why it was especially the low-income countries that advocated schemes for the stabilization of commodity prices, and also why they are rather disappointed that so far very little has been real-

* Let me add here that I have taken *all* countries for which data over the whole period were available.

Table 7.4
TRENDS IN EXPORTS, 1950-62

I	2 T	3 F	4 P
1. Uruguay	− 8.0	17.0	58
2. Colombia	− 0.5	12.0	77
3. Brazil	− 1.8	6.2	55
4. Chile	3.5	16.3	63
5. Argentina	0.9	7.4	18
6. Mexico	4.5	7.4	28
I Latin America	0.6	9.0	43
7. Nigeria	4.6	7.1	20
8. Cameroons	5.6	7.0	34
9. Ghana	3.0	6.4	66
II Africa South of Sahara	4.2	6.7	37
10. Indonesia	− 2.3	40.9	22
11. Malaya	1.7	16.6	62
12. Philippines	4.1	5.4	29
13. Ceylon	0.7	5.0	66
14. India	0.4	9.2	24
III Southeast Asia	0.8	15.4	37
15. Egypt	0.1	10.6	70
16. Turkey	0.3	9.4	34
IV Near East	0.2	10.0	52
17. V Australia	2.1	14.2	42
18. Sweden	6.7	6.3	16
19. Denmark	7.3	6.7	12
20. Netherlands	9.1	4.3	9
21. Belgium	6.4	7.6	22
22. United Kingdom	4.3	3.3	21
VI Western Europe	6.1	4.9	18
23. VII United States	4.7	9.5	17

T = exponential trend in exports in dollars (f.o.b.).
F = average annual percentage deviations from T.
P = percentage of total exports contributed by the most important commodity.

ized in this field. However, the low-income countries could well reproach themselves for having done so little until now to change their vulnerable export position into a somewhat stronger one. Here one has to repeat what has already been mentioned a few times before—it is characteristic of traditional societies that they attempt to continue with their customary modes of living even when circumstances have so altered that they are in contradiction with their whole sociocultural structure. It is exactly on these grounds that the writer considers price-stabilization schemes to be a conservative, even a reactionary approach to the development problem. By stabilizing the prices of primary commodities we run the risk of lulling the low-income countries by suggesting to them that their export problems are solved. But the only way really to solve them is through a greater diversification of their exports, and hence through industrialization. In order to demonstrate this thesis we have introduced a second explanatory variable—the percentage of total export revenue earned by the most important export commodity (Table 7.4, P). This variable has been introduced under the assumption that the lower this percentage, the greater the diversification of the exports and hence the greater the likelihood that with an unfavorable development in one of the export markets the country may find an escape in another.

We have thus computed the correlation between the numerical value of the trend of total export revenue T, and the average percentage fluctuations from this trend F, and the percentage of total exports in a single commodity P. Correlations have been computed for the seven economic-geographic areas as well as for the twenty-three individual countries. The following regression equations were obtained:

$$T_7 = 0.215\,F_7 - 0.129\,P_7 + 9.350$$
$$(R = 0.923)$$

$$T_{23} = 0.210\,F_{23} - 0.087\,P_{23} + 7.925$$
$$(R = 0.699)$$

Although the correlation is much weaker in the second case, it is interesting to observe that the coefficients are more or less the same. For the average values it was found that

	7 Areas	23 Countries
$\dfrac{dT}{dF} \cdot \dfrac{F}{T}$	— 0.803	— 0.866
$\dfrac{dT}{dP} \cdot \dfrac{P}{T}$	— 1.697	— 1.310

Hence we may conclude that if the percentage fluctuations of export revenues from their trends decrease by 1 per cent, the numerical value of the trend itself will increase by about 0.8 per cent, and that if the percentage of export revenue in a single commodity decreases by 1 per cent, the numerical value of the trend of export revenues will increase by a percentage of the magnitude of about 1.5.

Our numerical findings thus are in complete harmony with the statement made before—namely, that diversification of exports, i.e., industrialization, is of much greater importance for the single-commodity exporters than the stabilization of export prices. A percentage change in the diversification of the exports will have about twice as much effect on the change in the export trend than an equal percentage change in export revenue fluctuations.

CLOSING THE GAP

It was our intention to demonstrate in this book that the most difficult situation a government may have to face is to break through a Malthusian low per capita income equilibrium. We have seen that this is not only an economic problem but that fundamental overall social change is necessary in order to set in motion a process of economic development. In this last chapter we have seen however that industrialization, being one of the most important elements of economic development, encounters at least two difficulties in low-income countries: the long-term increase in their export revenues is low (and sometimes even negative) whereas these revenues—and therefore also the capacity to import—show huge annual fluctuations. Thus, longterm development plans are repeatedly threatened by the impossibility of importing the capital goods needed to realize the plans. Especially in those countries where the rapid increase in population absorbs practically the entire increase in national income, nothing is left with which to improve the welfare of the population. In those countries, one has, like the Red Queen mentioned earlier, to run fast in order to stay in the same place. And it is a race full of hurdles.

We have seen that many countries have not yet succeeded in shifting their economies from a largely agrarian basis to an industrial one. In order to succeed three main hurdles have to be overcome: the obstacles standing in the way of an increase in the propensity to invest; the difficulties hampering any extension of the supply of skilled labor and organizational talent; and the factors resisting a greater diversification of exports, thus preventing any diminishing of the fluctuations in the capacity to import.

It is precisely during the first period of industrialization, or as we have termed it, during the period of economic development that the governments of low-income countries have to face the greatest organizational and political problems. And it is during that period that they most urgently require the help of the richer members of the family of nations.

When in the early fifties economists became aware of the urgent need for a solution of the problems of low-income countries, within a short time they made available a group of theories to guide policy makers. The Harrod-Domar model was used to demonstrate that poor countries remained poor because they were not able to invest enough. The big push theory of Rosenstein-

Rodan showed that a *huge* increase in investment was needed to break through to low per capita income equilibrium, whereas the take-off theory of Rostow demonstrated that foreign aid might not be needed for a period longer than twenty years, because such a period would be sufficiently long to change a stagnant economy into a progressing one.

At the moment, however, the shortage of capital is no longer the greatest bottleneck in the development of low-income countries. On the contrary, many financial institutions in the rich countries complain that they would invest much more in low-income countries were satisfactory projects available. We have indicated that a low propensity to invest is understandable, especially when the political situation in a country is uncertain. But we may also state as a general rule that the lack of organizational ability, and the lack of skilled labor in general are frustrating the realization of development plans much more than the lack of capital. It is for this reason that in the last years more and more emphasis has been given to the education and training of managers and skilled laborers.

Last but not least we have demonstrated that many of the low-income countries are badly in need of short-term stand-by credit in order to overcome occasional balance of payments difficulties. Hence the rich countries have to develop a harmonious aid policy for the developing countries: technical assistance to help set up and implement plans and projects, capital imports to help finance them, and stand-by credits, if needed, in order to overcome unforeseen and undesirable balance of payments difficulties. We do not believe that such a proposal will be regarded as over-ambitious provided it is remembered that its purpose is to bring freedom from fear and hunger in the poor countries of our world community.

NOTES

1. W. W. Rostow, *The Process of Economic Growth* (1953), p. 11.

2. H. Myint, "The Gains from International Trade and the Backward Countries," *Review of Economic Studies*, 1954, pp. 129-142.

3. G. Haberler, "Some Problems in the Pure Theory of International Trade," *Economic Journal*, 1950, pp. 223-240.

4. Compare B. Lindner, *An Essay on Trade and Transformation* (1961), p. 27.

5. P. Lamartine Yates, *Forty Years of Foreign Trade* (1959), p. 180.

6. Compare P. Lamartine Yates, *op. cit.*, p. 178.

7. Compare R. Lekachman (ed.), *National Policy of Economic Welfare at Home and Abroad* (1955), p. 277.

8. From Food and Agricultural Organization, *Produits Agricole—Projections pour 1970* (1962), Tables M_1, M_4, and Table 5.

9. Compare P. Lamartine Yates, *op. cit.*, pp. 129, 135, 138, 145.

10. R. Prebisch, "The Role of Commercial Policies in Underdeveloped Countries," *American Economic Review* (Papers and Proceedings), May 1959; H. Singer, "The Distribution of Gains Between Investing and Borrowing Countries," *American Economic Review* (Papers and Proceedings), May 1950.

11. They are often, although not always correctly, identified with low-income countries. Compare C. P. Kindleberger, the *Terms of Trade* (1956), p. 262.

12. This thesis was indeed defended by J. M. Keynes in "Return of Estimated Value of Foreign Trade of the United Kingdom at Prices of 1900," *Economic Journal*, 1912, p. 631.

13. Compare "The Principal Problems of Economic Development of Latin American Countries," United Nations, 1950, p. 12.

14. H. Singer, *op. cit.*, p. 479.

15. B. Higgins, *op. cit.*, p. 368.

16. *Ibid.*, p. 361.

Studies in Economics

Studies in Political Science

Original studies on vital topics in the field of government and politics, attractively bound in sturdy paper covers.

Studies in Sociology

General Editorial Adviser: Charles H. Page,
Princeton University

Consulting Editor: Herbert A. Bloch, *Brooklyn College of the City University of New York*

A series of original studies on a large number of vital topics in the field of sociology, attractively bound in sturdy paper covers. Priced from 95¢ to $1.95.

Studies in Psychology

Studies in Philosophy

———————

J